The *INTRA*faith Co[r]
How Do Christians [T]
Ourselves About *INTER*faith Matters?

Susan M. Strouse, D.Min.

THE INTRAFAITH CONVERSATION
How Do Christians Talk Among Ourselves About
INTERfaith Matters
by Susan M. Strouse

Edited by Megan Rohrer

Cover Design by Megan Rohrer

First Printing

ISBN: 978-1-329-98352-6

For Elsie Leary

INTRODUCTION

"I'm worried that I'm betraying Jesus." - Elsie L.

What is an *intra*faith conversation and how is it different from an *inter*faith one? The simplest way to explain it is that the prefix matters. "Inter" means "between," "among," "in the midst of," "mutually," "reciprocally," "together." So *inter*faith is different religions being together. "Intra," on the other hand, means "within, inside, on the inside." *Intra*faith is one religion examining itself in light of its *inter*faith experience.

The conversation begins when we ask ourselves: what does it mean to be a Christian in our religiously diverse society today? This is not merely an academic question. In my experiences in both congregational ministry and interfaith dialogue, I have come to appreciate the people "on the ground" who wrestle with the implications of openness to other religions and how this affects their own beliefs and practices.

The idea for this book took root in the research project for my doctoral thesis, in which a group of Christians and Buddhists met together for six months to learn about one another and explore what impact the stories of people of a different tradition might have on their own.

But the seeds of my desire to create a user-friendly process for *inter*faith and *intra*faith engagement were planted much earlier. In the days after 9/11, many congregations wanted to learn about other religions. At North Park Lutheran Church in Buffalo, NY, where I was serving as pastor, our adult forum decided to begin a study of the world's religions. Emotions after the World Trade Center attacks were still raw. There were several people in the group who were not ready to begin the series with Islam, so they decided on Hinduism as their first venture into an interfaith encounter.

In light of the fact that we would be looking at another tradition solely through our own lenses, I asked the group if they would be open to inviting a Hindu guest to one of our sessions, someone who was willing to share her story as well as answer any questions. Their answer was an enthusiastic "yes" and I invited a

Hindu woman who was active in interfaith activities to come to our next meeting. The visit went well. The Christian participants were welcoming and respectful. They asked insightful questions.

However, after the session one of the participants, Elsie, asked if she could stay and talk about something that was bothering her. She began by saying how much she was enjoying the study. She had appreciated meeting our guest and hearing her personal story. But she had a big concern. "If I accept the Hindu path as equal to Christianity," she said, "I'm worried that I'm betraying Jesus." She also expressed her fear that she was breaking the commandment against chasing after other gods.

Elsie had presented me with both a pastoral and a theological quandary. I dealt with the pastoral concern immediately. I reassured her that, given her firm foundation in Christianity, an exploration of other faiths would not endanger her soul. Afterwards, however, when I reflected on the incident, I realized that Elsie had raised an important theological issue for Christians today.

Elsie's worry about "betraying Jesus" by meeting and respecting a person of another religion confronts us all with the question raised by Marjorie Suchoki in *Divinity and Diversity*: "How do Christians deal with this phenomenon?

> Our Christian past has traditionally taught us that there is only one way to God, and that is through Christ. But we are uneasy. Our neighborliness teaches us that these others are good and decent people, good neighbors, or loved family members! Surely God is with them as well as with us. Our hearts reach out, but our intellectual understanding draws back. We have been given little theological foundation for affirming these others – and consequently we wonder if our feelings of acceptance are perhaps against the will of God, who has uniquely revealed to us just what is required for salvation.[1]

---

[1] Suchocki, Marjorie, *Divinity & Diversity: A Christian Affirmation of Religious Pluralism.* Nashville: Abingdon Press, 2003, 9.

As pastors and lay leaders we are responsible to our congregations to provide the theological foundation for affirming "these others." Rather than succumbing to what John Cobb calls "the danger that sensitive Christians will simply delete central beliefs rather than transform them,"[2] I believe that we have some serious theological and Christological work to do in defining, or perhaps re-defining, ourselves in light of our *inter*faith milieu.

The good news is that there is a great deal being written and discussed at the academic level; books, essays and articles by theologians and biblical scholars abound. However, an exclusively academic approach will not suffice for a task that enters so deeply into the life and religious identity of all Christians. My intention in this book is to provide a practical approach as a parish pastor. To do this, I will 1) relate stories from my own evolving journey; 2) share accounts from people I've met in congregations, workshops, retreats and other circumstances; 3) ask questions to help you reflect on your own situation; and 4) offer resources that might help you in your own setting. While I will not go into great theological detail, this book can easily be used in conjunction with more academic resources for those who want to explore in more depth.

My intended audience is intentionally somewhat broad: from lay members of congregations with little or no theological training to seminarians and clergy with extensive theological backgrounds, albeit not necessarily in this area. Some sections may seem more academic, others more practical. I hope that you will read with this in mind. If a difficult section engenders lively discussion, my goal has been accomplished.

Since my first struggling attempt to answer Elsie's question, I have been following a quest to learn and grow in my own understanding of my faith in relationship to those with different beliefs and practices. After seventeen years of parish ministry, I left Western NY to pursue a Doctor of Ministry degree in interfaith studies at the Pacific School of Religion in Berkeley, CA. I also became actively involved with the Interfaith Center at the Presidio in San Francisco and served as interim executive director in 2011-12. I am still a parish pastor, over eleven years now at First United

[2] Cobb, John, *Lay Theology*. St. Louis: Chalice Press, 1994, 96.

Lutheran Church in San Francisco. I am blessed to serve a congregation which loves to explore matters of *inter*faith and *intra*faith as much as I do. They have been willing partners in this quest and I am grateful for their willingness to stretch and grow.

I hope that you will find this book helpful. Many people who become involved in interfaith activities say that meeting and learning about other religious traditions transforms their rootedness in their own tradition and makes it stronger. This has certainly been true for me. I hope it will be so for you.

PART I Why the *Intra*faith Conversation Is Necessary

Interreligious dialogue is today unavoidable; it is a religious imperative and a historical duty for which we must suitably prepare. – Raimon Panikkar[3]

*Inter*faith dialogues and activities are happening all around, which is laudable. What is largely missing, however, is conversation *among Christians* about what to do with the proverbial elephant in the Christian living room – Jesus Christ as the only way to salvation. Many see only a choice between fundamentalism (emphasizing the literally interpreted Bible as fundamental to Christian life and teaching)[4] and relativism (believing that different things are true, right, etc., for different people or at different times).[5]

While some cling to texts such as "There is no salvation in anyone else, for there is no other name under heaven given to the human race by which we must be saved,"[6] others dismiss their exclusivism by claiming, "But we're all worshipping the same God!"

Who is right? Taking a hard line position on either side will make dialogue difficult. Those who take the biblical witness literally will need to listen to those who have different interpretations or understandings. Those who are more accepting of other religions will need to hear about differences, the beliefs and practices that can cause disagreements among them.

To continue the quote above by Raimon Panikkar, one of the greatest scholars of comparative religion in the 20th century:

> I would like to begin by stressing the often-neglected notion of an intrareligious dialogue, i.e., an inner dialogue within myself, an encounter in the depth of my personal religiousness, having met another religious experience on that very intimate level. In other words,

---

[3] Panikkar, Raimon, *The Intrareligious Dialogue.* New York: Paulist, 1978, 40.

[4] *Merriam-Webster Dictionary.* s.v "fundamentalism," accessed February 26, 2016, http://www.merriam-webster.com/dictionary/fundamentalism.

[5] *Merriam-Webster Dictionary.* s.v "relativism," accessed February 26, 2016, http://www.merriam-webster.com/dictionary/relativism.

[6] *The Inclusive Bible,* Acts 4:12.

if interreligious dialogue is to be real dialogue, an intrareligious dialogue must accompany it.[7]

This section will begin to open the door to that dialogue. Reflection questions will follow each chapter.

---

[7] Ibid.

Chapter 1   The Interfaith Landscape

All of us live in the new world in which the proximity and intermingling of people of many faiths is a fact of our global life and increasingly our local lives as well. – Diana Eck[8]

Our society is increasingly diverse. There is no denying it. We used to say we were a melting pot, but now we recognize that we are more like a salad bowl or a mosaic of many races, cultures and religions. It is rare for someone to have no experience encountering a person of another religious tradition, if only on a superficial level. Members of our congregations have friends, neighbors, co-workers and family members from other religions. Our children go to school with children of other traditions. Intermarriages are more and more common. An increasing number of people are comfortable adhering to more than one tradition at the same time, while others identify as interspiritual.[9] The Internet has made isolation and ignorance of one another virtually impossible.

At a workshop at a Lutheran synod assembly, I opened by inviting people to think about a time when they had had an experience that involved a different religious tradition. It could have been a positive experience or a negative one. It might have been a celebratory occasion or one that had raised troubling questions. It might have involved just one person or a group. In a room of over fifty people, there was not one person who could not recall at least one encounter.[10] I then invited everyone to find a partner and share their experiences. The noise level in the room echoed the enthusiasm with which they told one another their stories.

Granted, this took place in California's multicultural Bay Area. But it could have taken place almost anywhere in the country, which has become much more aware of different religions both globally and

---

[8] Eck, Diana, "Honest to God: The Universe of Faith" in *God at 2000*, edited by Marcus Borg and Ross Mackenzie, Harrisburg, PA: Morehouse Pub., 2000, 43.

[9] The term "interspirituality" was coined by the late Wayne Teasdale, author of *The Mystic Heart*, who believed that spirituality is at the heart of all the world religions. A shared spiritual heritage enables us to go beyond the differences in our theological beliefs and traditions.

[10] I must add the disclaimer that one woman's experience was a Lutheran/Catholic encounter, which illustrates my point later that we have to meet people where they are.

locally. The interfaith landscape is becoming more developed every day. It is hard to imagine anyone being completely unaware of the different religions and traditions all around them.

At the global level, we have unfortunately become accustomed to hearing a lot of bad news. We deplore sectarian violence, such as Christians and Muslims killing each other in the Central African Republic and Buddhists massacring Muslims in Myanmar and Sri Lanka. We grieve at the chaos engendered by the hatred between Sunni and Shi'a. Sadly, in these examples, religion has played a big role in international news.

But interfaith organizations are also working worldwide to build bridges and overcome religious challenges to peace. These efforts receive very little press. The United Religions Initiative (URI),[11] for instance, is a network that connects people across religions and cultures. It supports initiatives for peace and justice all over the world. Hundreds of its cooperation circles[12] are in operation, ranging from bringing together Israelis and Palestinians in the Holy Land to addressing ecological issues in Latin America. Also, many major metropolitan areas today have Interreligious Councils that foster dialogue and joint work in social justice. These organizations, thankfully, have become part of the global interfaith landscape. They remind us that diversity does not have to be a cause of violence and

---

[11] URI was the brainchild of California Episcopal Bishop William Swing. In 1993, he received an invitation by the United Nations to host a large interfaith service at Grace Cathedral in San Francisco, marking the 50th anniversary of the signing of the UN Charter. Bishop Swing asked himself, "If the nations of the world are working together for peace through the UN, then where are the world's religions?"

[12] Cooperation Circles (CCs) are independently organized, self-governing and self-funding groups. These groups range from a minimum of seven members to tens of thousands, each representing at least three faiths or traditions, including the non-religious. Each subscribes to the shared vision outlined in URI's Charter and are connected to one another and the global URI network through regional anchor points, where regional coordinators help CCs build capacity, organize regional gatherings and trainings, and seed new CCs.

strife. And they encourage us to participate in projects of both cooperation and celebration in our own local landscape.

The Christian community is an integral part of this landscape. Once upon a time it could be argued that Christianity was *the* religion of the United States. Being Christian was the norm; the only differences we recognized were among Catholics and different denominations of Protestants. In the town where I was raised, I was marginally aware that there were "others." My only contact with Buddhism was by way of learning that the mother of a schoolmate, who had been born in China, had converted from Buddhism to Christianity. I had a few Jewish classmates, but I can't remember ever talking about or learning Jewish customs. Christian beliefs, language, art, and holidays were not questioned. They were taken for granted; it was simply the air we breathed.

Today, in most of the United States, this kind of predominance is quickly vanishing. Along with Christmas and Easter, there are prominent observations of Hanukkah, Ramadan, Dewali, Solstice and other sacred days. The annual kerfuffle over community Nativity displays or combinations of Christmas trees and menorahs is simply an indication of the anxiety engendered in some by our changing landscape. Even if we all agreed to say "Merry Christmas" instead of "Happy Holidays," we will never go back to the days of being a "Christian nation."

As a nation, we are confronted with a wide variety of religions and practices. Diana Eck, founder and director of the Pluralism Project at Harvard University, describes the environment in which we live today. In her book, *A New Religious America: How a 'Christian Country' Has Become the World's Most Religiously Diverse Nation*, she tells of her own journey into the new America:

> For ten years I have gone out looking for the religious neighbors of a new America. As a scholar, I have done the social equivalent of calling up and inviting myself, a stranger, to dinner. I have celebrated the Sikh New Year's festival of Baisakhi with a community in Fairfax, Virginia. I have feasted at the Vietnamese Buddhist "Mother's Day" in a temple in Olympia, Washington, and I have delivered an impromptu speech on the occasion of Lord Ram's Birthday at a new Hindu

temple in Troy, Michigan.[13]

The opportunities for the kinds of experiences Eck describes are endless. We should all be encouraged to get to know the new religious landscape in which we live. But despite many more examples of neighbors getting to know one another, it is my experience that many people in our congregations are not so bold as to "invite themselves to dinner." We stay in our own little enclaves of Lutheran, Presbyterian, etc. Even when we have joint meetings with other denominations, we tend to stick with the people we know.

This is not to say that interfaith work is not happening. Interfaith and interreligious[14] councils exist in all parts of the country. People of different religions are organizing themselves around civic projects, such as homelessness and hunger; justice issues such as human rights; and peace building. Here in San Francisco, the Interfaith Council has partnered with other local agencies since 1988 to operate the Interfaith Winter Shelter. They are also part of a disaster preparedness initiative to teach congregations how to respond to a natural or human-made disaster.

Interfaith Power & Light promotes energy conservation and efficiency as a religious response to global warming. Clergy and Laity United for Economic Justice (CLUE CA) is a statewide alliance of interfaith organizations whose aim is to end low-wage poverty in California. San Francisco Organizing Project/Peninsula Interfaith

---

[13] Diana L. Eck, *A New Religious America: How a "Christian Country" Has Become the World's Most Religiously Diverse Nation.* San Francisco: HarperSanFrancisco, 2001, 2.

[14] There is much ongoing discussion about what to call the movement. The Rev. Dr. Andrew Kille, executive director of the Silicon Valley Interreligious Council (SiVIC) writes that "interfaith carries some muddy implications that can be confusing - 'interfaith' organizations in the past meant 'ecumenical'- all Christian, or, at best, Christian/ Jewish. It has also come to describe traditions that blend two or more religious observances into some whole. We chose 'interreligious' partly because the term is less familiar, partly because it suggests relationships between distinct traditions, rather than a blending of them. Multi-faith has much the same kind of sense about it. 'Interreligious' is also a term that hopes to include traditions for whom 'faith' is not really a meaningful concept- Buddhists, Wiccans, etc." Interfaith? Multi-faith? Interreligious? Multi religious? Pan-spiritual? Religio-pluralistic? For the purpose of this book, I will usually use 'interfaith.'

Action develops community leaders and grassroots campaigns around issues like health care, affordable housing, neighborhood safety, economic opportunities and education. Interfaith cooperation abounds! And many congregations and individual members are active in these initiatives.

The Pluralism Project has now undertaken the task of documenting the development of these councils and coalitions - what they call the "interfaith infrastructure" of the United States. The twenty cities they have selected for the project range from Spokane, WA to Richmond, VA and from Jacksonville, FL to Wichita, KS. It is clear that interfaith alliances are here to stay. They provide an important way for us to "invite ourselves to dinner" and partake of the richness of what our world has to offer.

From the stories told by the participants in my workshops and on many other occasions, we see that engagement in interfaith thinking is happening on the personal level as well. These engagements and thoughts may stimulate a lot of questions. But these questions are a critical component of our landscape.

The Christian church should be providing resources, tools, opportunities and support for its adherents to navigate the terrain and to live faithfully in this beautifully diverse land. There are many resources available to get an overview of the world's religions. That is not the purpose of this book. In the chapters that follow, I hope, rather, that you will find a map to guide you on your way – both in reaching outward to your neighbors of other faiths, and in reaching inward to your own understanding of what it means to be a Christian in an interfaith world.

FOR REFLECTION:

Think about a time when you had a personal experience that involved a person or persons of a different religious tradition.

- What was that experience like for you?
- What were your impressions of the person(s) of the other religion?
- What questions, if any, did the encounter raise for you?

How has the fact of the religious diversity of the United States made an impact?

- On you?
- Your family?
- Your community?
- Your church?

Do you know if there is an interfaith council or coalition in your area?

- If so, what do you know about it?
- Have you or your church been involved in any way? Could you be?

SUGGESTED READING:

- *A New Religious America: How a 'Christian Country' Has Become the World's Most Religiously Diverse Nation* by Diana Eck[15]

---

[15] Eck, Diana, *A New Religious America: How a 'Christian Country' Has Become the World's Most Religiously Diverse Nation.* San Francisco: HarperSanFrancisco, 2001.

Chapter 2   The Intrafaith Landscape: A New Reformation

About every five hundred years the Church feels compelled to hold a giant rummage sale. -Bishop Mark Dyer

Like it or not, change is also happening within American Christianity. New ways of being church are springing up all around. Unlike the "worship wars" of previous decades, which pitted traditional and contemporary proponents against one another, the movement today is not so easy to classify. Terms such as "emergent," "post-denominational," "post-modern" and "progressive" attempt to describe the Christian scene and the movements going on within it. Each of these categorizations contains within itself a wide variety of interpretations of what it really means.

All of these are taking part in a "giant rummage sale," as Bishop Dyer so brilliantly describes it. However, it is clear that we are not all in agreement about what we should keep and what we should give away. Perhaps it would be more accurate to say that we are in the process of getting ready for the rummage sale. If you have ever held a yard, garage or rummage sale, you know the work that goes into putting it together. The first thing you have to do is look over all of your stuff with a critical eye. As you look at each cherished possession, you ask: Do I want to keep this? Is it still useful? Does it still fit? Does it still work? If the answer is 'yes,' the decision is easy; it's a keeper. And if 'no,' to the sale it goes.

It gets a bit more complicated when you have an item that is tarnished, worn or outdated but you think there just might be some life left in it. You have to ask yourself if maybe, if it were cleaned up, restored or reworked, it could still be of value to you. A dusty old heirloom might just turn out to be a new treasure.

So it is in present-day Christianity. We are looking with critical eyes at social issues, liturgical forms, biblical interpretations, theological teachings and the use of language. However not all churches necessarily deal with all of these, nor would they all agree. For example, a few years ago I attended, along with some members of my current congregation, a conference on the emerging church. First United considers itself to be a progressive congregation, committed to the use of inclusive language for humanity and expansive language for

God. At First United's rummage sale, we had examined patriarchal language and decided that it had to go. So we were quite surprised by the lack of inclusive language used at the conference and by the fairly orthodox theology. We realized that we are all making different value judgment about our treasures. This is the reformation that is happening all around us. Old ideas are being reexamined, transformed or rejected; new ones are emerging.

Why is all this change happening now? Taking her cue from Bishop Dyer, the late Phyllis Tickle posited that we are in this current "giant rummage sale" simply because it's time for one. In *The Great Emergence: How Christianity Is Changing and Why*[16], she outlined the upheaval that has occurred every five hundred years since the time of Jesus. The Protestant Reformation began in the 16th century. The 11th century saw the Great Schism, which split the Eastern and Western Churches. In the 6th century, the Roman Empire collapsed and Europe entered the Dark Ages. All of these upheavals included both societal shifts and theological issues, just like we are experiencing now in the 21st century.

What I find most helpful about Tickle's theory is that what we're going through is normal. That means we can go about being creative and hopeful, rather than hidebound and anxious. This is good news because the church has been anxiety-driven for quite a while. Our outreach efforts have been fueled by the decline in membership in Christian congregations. Pundits have been writing ad nauseam about the reasons for this. The latest trend is expounding on the characteristics of the Millennial generation and how the church can reach out and reel them in. Some of these same "experts" also tell us how to appeal to those who are "spiritually independent" (a more positive way of saying "spiritual but not religious" or "none") all around us.

Don't misunderstand me: I am all in favor of doing outreach to those searching for a way to explore their spirituality and to those with no church home. However, as a veteran of the church growth movement of the 1990s, I know the pitfalls of easy characterizations and easy solutions. The experts told us then that we had to adapt to

---

[16] Tickle, Phyllis, *The Great Emergence: How Christianity Is Changing and Why*. Grand Rapids, MI. Baker Books, 2008.

the needs of Generation X and that if we would just follow their instructions to the letter, our churches would grow. We actually bought a program like this in my former congregation. We received a big binder of step-by-step instructions - and a church growth consultant! We envisioned our little congregation in a Northeast rustbelt city growing by 200-400%.

Looking back, the idea was ludicrous. We were a mainline church in a city itself in decline. But even more ludicrous was the advice of our "expert" consultant. He took one look at our building, sitting on the corner in the middle of two lovely lawns with large shade trees, and declared that we needed to rip out the trees and the laws and put in parking lots. Rule #1 of church growth: you have to have a parking lot. Needless to say, we did not tear up the lawns. They provided play space for our preschool and summer program. They were places of hospitality for neighborhood gatherings, such as the annual National Night Out. The trees provided shade and beauty, as well as nesting places for birds. We were a green space in a city neighborhood. Should we really have "paved Paradise and put up a parking lot.?"[17]

I am happy to report that the congregation is still there, some twenty years after our venture into church growth. The congregation is still small, but they have partnered with a congregation in the suburbs and are doing vibrant, creative ministry together. When I returned for their 90th anniversary celebration last year, one of the things I enjoyed most was the cookout held out on the back lawn under that big beautiful tree.

Despite my obvious feelings about the experience, I learned an important lesson: there are no one-size-fits-all answers to the questions of doing ministry in different settings. Another thing that I learned from the traditional/ contemporary worship wars is that for many the rummage sale included only musical styles, not language and theology. For instance, the popular contemporary Christian song "Forever"[18] includes the lyrics

---

[17] Mitchell, Joni, "Big Yellow Taxi," Reprise Records. 1970.
[18] Tomlin, Chris, "Forever," sixstepsrecords, 2001.

Give thanks to the Lord
Our God and King
His love endures forever
For He is good, He is above all things
His love endures forever

This one hits the trifecta: exclusively male pronouns, hierarchical imagery for God ("Lord," "King") and an outdated view of a three-tiered universe ("above all things").

Not that this is limited to recent contemporary music. One song, written in 1966, brought the *inter*faith/*intra*faith issue home to me. One of my favorite songs that we often sang at the contemporary service at my former congregation was "I Am the Bread of Life."[19] I never had any problem in singing it with gusto. That is until I sat with Kitty at a funeral. I knew Kitty from a women's interfaith group, so when I saw her at a funeral at a neighboring Episcopal church, I sat next to her. As the priest read the familiar passage from John's gospel, I heard it through the ears of my friend who is Jewish: "I am the Way, the Truth and the Life; no one comes to the Father but by me." I was God-smacked. I had preached on that same text many times, but hearing it this time was such a powerful epiphany that I didn't want to go up to receive Holy Communion. It felt rude, exclusionary, and offensive. The next time we sang the song I almost choked. I could not sing these lyrics:

Unless you eat of the flesh of the Son of Man
And drink of his blood, you shall not have life within you.

That revelation widened for me a quest that had previously been one of *inter*faith exploration. I had been happily content to meet people who followed other paths, but I had not been confronted with the *intra*faith question. But once it entered into my consciousness, I had no choice. I had to look with a critical eye at my belief in Jesus as the only way to salvation and make a decision about whether to keep

---

[19] Toolan, Sister Suzanne ,"I Am the Bread of Life,", GIA Publications, 1966.

it, give it away or transform it into something new. And if I wanted to transform it into something new, how could I do that with faithfulness and integrity?

I will be honest. The process of transformation is not necessarily quick and easy. Just look at previous reformations. The Protestant Reformation lasted over a century and is filled with violent clashes over theological matters such as infant baptism. The theological disputes that the Great Schism created spanned centuries. There were many other elements involved, to be sure. Societal and political factors played key roles as well. As they do today. We do our theology in the midst of a changing world and changing social norms. Some day we will look back and wonder why we spent as much time on issues like the ordination of women and LGBTQ people as theologians of the Great Schism debated the hot topic of whether the Holy Spirit proceeded from the Father or from the Father and the Son.

Issues may change. Culture may change. The task of the church is to live out "ecclesia semper reformanda est" ("the church is always to be reformed").[20] In reaching out to Millenials, spiritual independents, the "church alumni society[21]," we must take up the challenge in our own time. The inclusion of *inter*faith and *intra*faith is an essential part of living out this challenge.

Imagine, then, my delight in arriving at the Graduate Theological Union in Berkeley to work on my doctorate in this area and discovering a course entitled *Martin Luther and Buddhism*![22] In the class I became immersed in a fascinating convergence of Lutheran and Buddhist teaching. I was mainly interested in learning about a tradition other than mine. After all, I knew about Lutheranism. But to my surprise, the primary benefit of the course for me was an invigorating renewal of Luther's theology of the cross. Through study of the Buddhist concept of dukka (suffering), I was able to reimagine the central symbol of Christianity that I had not been sure I could espouse any longer. My rummage sale item could still be a keeper.

---

[20] Attributed to Karl Barth.
[21] Phrase coined by Bishop John Shelby Spong to describe those who have left the church.
[22] Chung, Paul S, *Martin Luther and Buddhism: Aesthetics of Suffering*. Wipf & Stock Publishers. Eugene, OR. 2002.

You see, the reformation process is not only about the above-mentioned groups. As the story in my introduction illustrates, active members of congregations, like Elsie and people of all ages (Elsie was in her 70s at the time) want to know how to navigate this "rummage sale" process. And my own story of being a 60-something parish pastor reclaiming her Lutheran identity in an interfaith context demonstrates a way forward for clergy.

Because if we are going to be part of this new reformation and we are serious about relating to people of all ages in our congregations and to the spiritually independents, then the *inter*faith/*intra*faith conversation must be part of our ministry.

FOR REFLECTION:

- What do you think about Bishop Dyer's statement: "About every five hundred years the Church feels compelled to hold a giant rummage sale."?
- Do you agree with Phyllis Tickle that we are in such a situation today?
- What is an aspect of the Church that you would like to give away?
- What do you definitely want to keep?
- What are some components that you think might be redeemable with some work?

SUGGESTED READING:

- *The Great Emergence: How Christianity Is Changing and Why* by Phyllis Tickle[23]

---

[23] Tickle, Phyllis, *The Great Emergence.*

Chapter 3   New Voices

I'd like to suggest that many of the Nones have "gotten off the bus," an expression that refers to travelers who want to escape pre-packaged tourism so that they can discover a place as it "really" is. - Anne Benvenuti[24]

We in the church must accept the fact that, for many people, the old categories of Catholic/Protestant, Episcopal/Methodist, high church/low church, contemporary/traditional, etc. just do not matter. There are new voices contributing to the religious scene, although most of them would not like to be referred to as religious. But as we go about our work of understanding our *inter*faith and *intra*faith context, these voices deserve to be heard. They may have left or never been part of the church, but that does not mean that they do not have a lot to say about spirituality, the meaning of life and how to make a difference in the world.

Spiritual Independents

People who are spiritually independent share the same existential questions as almost every human being but do not confine their search for answers to any one religion. – Rabbi Rami Shapiro[25]

A piece of accepted wisdom among many involved in interfaith dialogue is that one must first be grounded in one particular tradition. This is reflected in the quote by Mahatma Gandhi that ". . . our innermost prayer should be a Hindu should be a better Hindu, a Muslim a better Muslim, a Christian a better Christian."[26] However, according to the Pew Research Center, the number of Americans who do not identify with any religion continues to grow at a rapid pace. One fifth of the US public – and a third of adults under thirty – are religiously unaffiliated today, the highest percentages ever in Pew

[24] Benvenuti, Anne. "The Nones Are Off the Bus, and Many of Them are Alls." theinterfaithobserver. http://theinterfaithobserver.org/journal-articles/2013/5/15/the-nones-are-off-the-bus-and-many-of-them-are-alls.html (accessed February 26, 2016).

[25] Shapiro, Rami. *Perennial Wisdom for the Spiritually Independent.* Woodstock, VT: SkyLight Paths, 2013, Kindle edition, location 82.

[26] Gandhi, Mahatma, "Young India," January 19, 1928.

Research Center polling.[27]

We often refer to these folks as the "spiritual but not religious" or "Nones." But I agree with Rabbi Rami Shapiro, who has declared that these designations are too negative and has coined the more positive "spiritually independent." He says:

> Most of these so-called Nones are not dismissive of God or spirituality but simply find religious labels and affiliation too narrow and constraining. This is why I choose to call this segment of the population by the far more positive and accurate term spiritually independent.[28]

In another positive take on it, the Rev. Dr. Anne Benvenuti, a Board Trustee for the Council for a Parliament of the World's Religions, writes in "The Nones Are Off the Bus, and Many of Them are Alls:"

> I know a lot of Nones and many of them are Alls. They celebrate the Winter Solstice, and Easter sunrise, they may do yoga or meditate, and they give thoughtfully to charities, all in no particular order, but depending on where they are, how they feel, what seems to be called for. They resist labels produced by media-saturated culture to represent certain predetermined sets of characteristics. They distrust such prepackaged beliefs, and also distrust religious institutions that are so often corrupt and hypocritical. Yet they value human spiritual heritage, often in great variety, and many of these people are more comfortable in a variety of religious settings than they would be in only one.[29]

In the new emerging community being formed by Mission Developer, Pastor Anders Peterson under the sponsorship of my congregation, First United Lutheran Church, we are finding the truth

---

[27] "Nones" on the Rise." pewforum.org.
http://www.pewforum.org/2012/10/09/nones-on-the-rise/ (Accessed February 28, 2016).
[28] Shapiro, 82.
[29] Benvenuti, Anne.

of these perspectives. Mission, defined as converting people to Christianity, does not work with this group. Openness to other religious traditions is essential. This is not to say that we deny or water down who we are; we do our work in the world as Christians. But we do it as Christians who have worked through the *intra*faith questions that are raised by many as they are confronted with this population. According to the Rev. Bud Heckman, senior advisor to Religions for Peace USA in New York City:

> A couple of decades ago this category accounted for no more than a single-digit percentage of the population. Today it accounts for one of every five people in the States, and one in every three amongst those under 30 years of age. The numbers are even higher in Europe and China. This means there is a great deal of fluidity in identity that is socially permissible in ways that simply were not true before.[30]

We do not know what Mahatma Gandhi would make of our world today. However it is clear that, both within Christianity and on the interfaith scene, the spiritual independents must be part of the *inter*faith and *intra*faith conversations.

---

[30] Heckman, Bud, "Five Things Changing the Way Religions Interact." theinterfaithobserver. http://theinterfaithobserver.org/journal-articles/2013/12/15/five-things-changing-the-way-religions-interact.html (accessed February 26, 2016).

Hybrid Spirituality: Multiple Belonging

The phenomenon of "multiple religious belonging" is now deeply engrained in American Culture – Francis X. Clooney[31]

The first time I heard someone referred to as a Jewbu, I thought it was a pejorative term. But it is not. Jewbu (or Jubu or Bu-Jew) is simply is the abbreviation for a Jewish Buddhist. This fairly recent term can refer to either a Buddhist who grew up Jewish but no longer practices Judaism ("This is true of a staggeringly high percentage of American Buddhist leaders; well over half by most counts," according to Rabbi Julian Sinclair[32]) or a Buddhist who still practices and identifies with Judaism. Sylvia Boorstein, a founding teacher of Spirit Rock Meditation Center in Woodacre, CA, is a good example of this category. Her autobiographical memoir, *That's Funny, You Don't Look Buddhist: On Being a Faithful Jew and a Passionate Buddhist*[33], places her squarely in the camp of those with multiple belongings. Her story of coming to terms with her identity as both a Jew and a Buddhist – and her deepened love for Judaism – is an engaging, easy read for anyone wanting an introduction to this phenomenon.

Christianity does not have a catchy term to describe its hybrids (Chrisbu or Bu-Chris is just not as mellifluous as Jubu!). But there are those who are multiple belongers. For example, Father Gregory Mayers, coordinator of the East-West Meditation program at Mercy Center retreat center in Burlingame, CA, is both a Redemptorist priest and Associate Roshi of the Sanbô-Kyôdan Religious Foundation in Kamakura, Japan. Catholic theologian Paul Knitter, author of *Without Buddha I Could Not Be A Christian*,[34] considers himself to be an adherent of both Christianity and Buddhism.

It may be that the popularity of Buddhism has not caused a lot of consternation in our churches because Buddhism is not a theistic

---

[31] Clooney, Francis X., "New Wave Interreligious Thinking," americamagazine.org. http://americamagazine.org/content/all-things/new-wave-interreligious-thinking (accessed March 3, 2016).

[32] Sinclair, Rabbi Julian. "Jubu." thejc.com. http://www.thejc.com/judaism/jewish-words/jubu (accessed February 26, 2016).

[33] Boorstein, Sylvia. *That's Funny, You Don't Look Buddhist: On Being a Faithful Jew and a Passionate Buddhist.* San Francisco: HarperSanFrancisco, 1997.

[34] Knitter, Paul, *Without Buddha I Could Not Be a Christian.* Oxford: Oneworld, 2009.

religion (not all Buddhists would even call it a religion at all). But now we wade into deeper waters to examine more controversial examples of multiple belonging.

Many years ago a member of my congregation told me that she had become a Muslim. When I asked her how she reconciled that with being a Christian, she said that she saw no problems with it. At the time, I could not understand that. Now I see that she was merely ahead of her time. In 2007, an Episcopal priest named Ann Redding Holmes declared herself to be a Muslim after a profound experience of Muslim prayer. However, she did not abandon her Christian identity, saying that her acceptance of Islam was "not an automatic abandonment of Christianity. For many, it is. But it doesn't have to be."[35] In response to those who said that the two traditions are mutually exclusive, she said, "I just don't agree."[36] The Episcopal Church did not agree with her and she was defrocked in 2009. In interviews, Redding has argued that her views about Jesus "fit well in the range of Christianity."[37]

As strange as this story may seem, there are more and more examples of multiple belonging on the religious scene, as S. Wesley Ariarajah puts it, "throwing spanners into the smoothly oiled works of religious particularities."[38] But, reminding us that we are looking through Western lenses, he reports that multiple belonging is not a new phenomenon in North Asia:

---

[35] Tu, Janet I. "Episcopal Priest Ann Holmes Redding has been defrocked." seattletimes.com. http://seattletimes.com/html/localnews/2008961581_webdefrocked01m.html (accessed February 24, 2016).

[36] Ibid.

[37] Zimmerman, Cathy. "Ann Holmes, A Christian and a Muslim, to Share Message at St. Stephens." tdn.com http://tdn.com/lifestyles/ann-holmes-a-christian-and-a-muslim-to-share-message/article_de097bc0-1727-11e2-a92d-0019bb2963f4.html?print=true&cid=print (accessed February 24, 2016).

[38] Ariarajah, S. Wesley. "Religious Diversity and Interfaith Relations in a Global Age." flinders.edu.au. http://www.flinders.edu.au/oasis-files/chaplains/geoff_papers/ariarajah.pdf (accessed February 24, 2016).

It has been a common feature among the peoples especially in North Asia. Many of them have found ways of holding together two or more of religious traditions like Confucianism, Buddhism, Shintoism, Shamanism, Christianity etc. as tributaries that feed their overall religious consciousness and practice.[39]

Catherine Cornille, editor of *Many Mansions: Multiple Religious Belonging and Christian Identity* agrees:

It may be argued that . . . religion in Europe, America and Australia is just coming to terms with a practice or a form of religiosity that has been prevalent for ages in most of the rest of the world, and especially in the East.[40]

For many of our clergy and church members, learning how to relate to those who claim multiple belonging may seem to be a very steep learning curve. And to be honest, it is. It involves looking carefully at our assumptions about what it means to be a Christian, to listen to the stories of those who have different assumptions, and to participate in a religious quest that is ongoing and evolving.

For example, a member of my congregation admitted that she considered herself to be a Christian-Pagan. When I shared her story with a friend who is a Wiccan elder, he laughed and told me that Wicca is actually losing some of its appeal among disenfranchised Christians. Once, he said, Wicca was attractive to those looking for an earth-based, environment-friendly belief system and practice. But as Christianity has been slowly leaving behind its earth/spirit dualism and rediscovering its "roots" in theologians such as St. Francis of Assisi and Hildegard of Bingen, it is retaining some of those who in the past would have become Pagan. It is clearly a new day for Christianity!

---

[39] Ibid.
[40] Cornille, Catherine, ed. *Many Mansions? Multiple Religious Belonging and Christian Identity*. New York: Orbis Books, 2002, 1.

Atheists and Humanists

When I told the people of Northern Ireland that I was an atheist, a woman in the audience stood up and said, 'Yes, but is it the God of the Catholics or the God of the Protestants in whom you don't believe?"

- Quentin Crisp, The Wit and Wisdom of Quentin Crisp

It is all too common for those of us in the church to disregard people in these categories. We might dismiss them with "There are no atheists in foxholes" and similar sayings. And while I struggle to find ways of communicating my understandings of the Divine to those whose unbelief is more of a reaction to the abuses of church and religion, I also recognize that there are many good, thoughtful, moral people who do not feel the need for a Higher Power. Yet more and more of them are joining the interfaith conversation (you see why interfaith and interreligious are problematic terms!).

During the summer months, we welcome guests from different religious and non-religious traditions to speak at our church on a specific topic. Two years ago the subject was caring for creation. Most of our guests were easy to describe, e.g. Buddhist, Hindu, Jewish, Muslim. But one speaker, Chris Highland, was not so easy to categorize. He did not like using any labels at all, but finally settled on "free-thinking naturalist." Beginning his talk, he jokingly said that he had deliberately avoided the "A" word when referring to himself.

Atheism is a tricky subject. It used to be simple: an atheist was someone who didn't believe in God. Then many of us read or heard Marcus Borg (1942-2015) describe his many conversations with university students. He recounts,

> Every term, one or more of them says to me after class, 'This is all very interesting, but I have a problem every time you use the word 'God' because, you see'- here there's usually a pause and a deep breath- 'I really don't believe in God.' I always respond the same way: 'Tell me about the God you don't believe in.' [41]

---

[41] Borg, Marcus, *The Heart of Christianity. Christianity: Rediscovering a Life of Faith.* New York: HarperCollins, 2003, 68-69.

As Borg tells it, the student then describes a version of God perhaps learned in Sunday school, from parents or simply from popular culture. When Borg says, "Well, I don't believe in that God either,"[42] a space opens up for conversation about other possible ways of understanding the Divine.

As more people discover that there are other ways of thinking about their concept of God, the old definition of "not believing" becomes more problematic. Also, we are becoming more familiar with religions that are non-theistic (hence a-theistic), such as Buddhism, which has no concept of a creator God or divine intercessor. It is not so much that Buddhists do not believe in God (as if a conscious negative choice) as the fact that those are simply not aspects of their tradition.

Karen Armstrong has this to say:

Atheism is often a transitional state: Jews, Christians, and Muslims were all called atheists by their pagan contemporaries because they had adopted a revolutionary notion of divinity and transcendence. The people who have been dubbed atheists over the years have always denied a particular conception of the divine. But is the God who is rejected by atheists today the God of the patriarchs, the God of the prophets, the God of the philosophers, the God of the mystics, or the God of the eighteenth-century deists? All these deities have been venerated, but they are very different from one another. Perhaps modern atheism is a similar denial of a God that is no longer adequate to the problems of our time.[43]

Of course there are those who do not believe in any kind of Divine being, no matter how we might reimagine what that means. Many of these folks are also interested in being part of interreligious conversations. Henry Baer, a long-time member of the board at the Interfaith Center at the Presidio is a co-founder of an organization in

---

[42] Ibid.
[43] Roemischer, Jessica, "A New Axial Age: Karen Armstrong on the History—and the Future—of God."
http://www.adishakti.org/_/a_new_axial_age_by_karen_armstrong.htm (accessed February 26, 2016).

Berkeley called Ahimsa (the Sanskrit word meaning 'nonviolence'). One of the goals of the organization is "to encourage dialogues and public forums on issues which bridge spirituality and science and society."[44] Henry is also an avowed atheist, yet appreciates deeply the opportunity to work on projects together with others who want to be peacemakers in the world.

I contrast Chris and Henry with militant atheists, such as Richard Dawkins and Bill Maher, who denounce the God they don't believe in, but are never willing to listen to or discuss any other possibilities. I consider them to be as intractable as any fundamentalist of any religion.

I will admit that I never got the consternation that many Christians had about humanists (or as one elderly church member called them hoomanists). I thought humanists were pretty good people. I do now understand why they are considered by some to be fair game for Christian conversion: they value human agency and critical thinking over faith and doctrine. It could be said that humanism is a kinder, gentler atheism. As Nathan Phelps said, "What I am is a proud humanist. Atheism says what I don't accept, humanism says what I do."[45]

But these terms are very fluid. Another guest in our speaker series was Vanessa Gomez Brake, who is very involved in the interfaith scene and describes herself (at least for today, she said) as a Secular Humanist. However, she said that others have called her a "faitheist." This was the first I had heard of the term, which comes from the book *Faitheist: How an Atheist Found Common Ground with the Religious* by Chris Stedman.[46] Stedman's point is that atheists should be involved in respectful dialogue with those of religious persuasion. Vanessa said, however, that being called a "faitheist" was not a compliment. The Urban Dictionary defines it as "an atheist who is 'soft' on religious belief, and tolerant of even the worst intellectual and moral excesses of religion; an atheist accommodationist."[47] For

---

[44] http://ahimsaberkeley.org (accessed February 26, 2016).

[45] Nathan Phelps is the son of Westboro Baptist Church founder, Fred Phelps. He responded to my inquiry that this quote was something he had posted on Facebook and now has become a meme.

[46] Stedman, Chris, *How an Atheist Found Common Ground with the Religious*. Boston, MA: Beacon Press, 2012.

[47] *Urban Dictionary*, s.v. "faitheist,"
http://www.urbandictionary.com/define.php?term=faitheist (accessed February

some reason, it gives me satisfaction to know that there are factions even among the non-believers.

What I have learned from listening to those on the interfaith scene who describe themselves with the "A" word or with other isms is that these are people of good will and great love for humanity and the world. I welcome the opportunity to be in dialogue. Right now I have members in my congregation with family members who are declared atheists. I would love to have the "Tell me about the God you don't believe in" conversation with them – not in order to convince them that they are wrong, but to see where they really fit in the wide range of what atheism means today. And what "God" means today.

FOR REFLECTION:

- Do you know someone who would be considered spiritually independent? If so, have you had or could you have a conversation with that person about what they believe?
- Are you a spiritual independent? How would you describe your spirituality?

- What is your reaction to Anne Holmes Redding's and Father Gregory Mayers' stories? Are there differences between them? If so, what are they?
- Do you know someone who is a hybrid? If so, have you ever asked to hear the story of how she or he came to their multiple belonging?
- Are you yourself a hybrid? Have you ever told anyone your story? Why or why not? If you are not a hybrid, is there another religion you could conceivably adopt?

26, 2016).

Do you know someone who is an atheist? Have you ever had or could you have a conversation with him or her about what that means?

- How do you think it is possible for an atheist, agnostic or humanist can participate in interreligious dialogue?

SUGGESTED READING:

- *Saffron Cross: The Unlikely Story of How a Baptist Minister Married a Hindu Monk* by Dana Trent[48]
- "Welcoming the Spiritually Independent" Frederic and Mary Ann Brussat[49]
- *Perennial Wisdom for the Spiritually Independent* by Rami Shapiro[50]
- *Faitheist: How an Atheist Found Common Ground with the Religious* by Chris Stedman[51]

---

[48] Trent, Dana, *Saffron Cross: The Unlikely Story of How a Baptist Minister Married a Hindu Monk*. Nashville, TN: Fresh Air Books, 2013.

[49] Brussat, Frederic and Mary Ann, "Welcoming the Spiritually Independent." patheos.com.
http://www.patheos.com/blogs/dailylifeasspiritualpractice/2013/09/welcoming -the-spiritually-independent/ (accessed February 26, 2016).

[50] Shapiro, Rami.

[51] Stedman, Chris, *Faitheist: How an Atheist Found Common Ground with the Religious*. Boston: Beacon Press, 2012.

Chapter 4   A Question of Identity

I want to deal with questions of how one, as a Bible-tutored Christian, can come to think about God's whole menagerie and the place of the Christian Church and the Christian religion in the midst of it. – Krister Stendahl[52]

Way back in the 1980s, when I was doing my year of internship in a large Lutheran church, I had the opportunity to observe my supervisor conduct a rehearsal for a Jewish-Christian wedding. When the wedding party arrived, someone reminded my supervisor that he had agreed to remove the Paschal candle from the front of the church. I was appalled. I remember thinking, "But this is a Christian church; this is who we are. We shouldn't deny that!" I never mentioned it to my supervisor and missed an opportunity to discuss the issue. At the time, I was forming my own pastoral identity, steeped in "correct" theological beliefs and church practices, so I may not have been open to a more expansive view at that time. Decades later, however, I look back and see the question of identity as a crucial one with which the church of today must wrestle. It is part of the *inter*faith and *intra*faith landscapes. And it is an ongoing process! Even now, when officiating at a wedding at the chapel at the Interfaith Center at the Presidio, I flinch a little when we pull the drapes over the cross in the front of the church. It's like telling Jesus to turn his back for a little while.

Identity is important. How can I make my way in the world if I don't know who I am? If I am confused or if I allow myself to be swayed by someone with a stronger sense of self, I risk losing myself completely. Boundaries are a big part of identity. Part of an infant's

---

[52] Stendahl, Krister, "From God's Perspective We Are All Minorities." From a lecture delivered on February 27, 1992, at the Center for the Study of World Religions, Harvard University, as edited by Arvind Sharma and Jennifer Baichwal. Krister Stendahl (1921–2008) was a Swedish theologian and New Testament scholar, a professor and professor emeritus at Harvard Divinity School. He also served as Bishop of Stockholm in the Church of Sweden, Chair of the World Council of Churches' Consultation on the Church and the Jewish People, and as co-director of the Osher Center for Tolerance and Pluralism, Shalom-Hartman Institute in Jerusalem.

growth process is discovering where she ends and her mother and others begin. We have learned that poor boundaries lead to all kinds of dysfunction in individuals, families and organizations. So it is no wonder we become alarmed when we feel that our identity as Christians has been eroded. We feel threatened, under attack from all directions – secularism, science, a new generation that does not find the same meaning in the institutions in which we were raised.

And then there is the reality of religious diversity. Just look at the panicked responses to "the war on Christmas." My Facebook page this past season was filled with challenges to dare to say "Merry Christmas" instead of "Happy Holidays."

This anxiety is not unique to Christianity. Sylvia Boorstein, who is Jewish, reflects on the popularity of Buddhism:

> . . . I think the alarm people express about Buddhism has more to do with instinctive fears about tribal survival than philosophical error. . . Doing an action that another group does . . . arouses concern. I think it's the natural, self-protective, genetic response of tribes. [53]

Our Christian tribe is anxious. We lament the decline in membership in our churches and try to figure out how to attract new people. We worry about how to pay for the expenses of the staff, buildings and programs we've come to expect as necessary parts of being "church." We live in survival mode and when we can no longer afford these perceived necessities, we count ourselves as failures. Our churches are "no longer viable." That word has always reminded me of the names of Gomer's children in the book of Hosea: "Not loved," "Not my people." Talk about a dysfunctional family!

The interesting thing is that in Hosea the children's names are chosen by God as a expression of displeasure with the people for following false gods. Seen in this light, Elsie's concern about "chasing after false gods" was not for her self alone, but for the entire community.

---

[53] Boorstein, 135-6.

I believe that our tribe will be in trouble, not because of all the other tribes out there, but because we will not have figured out who we are in the midst of them. As an experiment I once asked members of a congregation what it means to be a Christian (this was a group with a high level of trust and willingness to have a spirited discussion). The first answer was, "It means being a good person." I pushed back a little and said that people of other faiths could be good people, too; in fact, atheists could be good people. "How then, do we identify ourselves as Christians?" I asked. I received a lot of blank stares. Please understand; I am not criticizing the group at all. When a tribe has been homogeneous, there has been no need to question its identity.

Of course, someone finally spoke up and said that we are Christians because we believe in Jesus. "Yes," I agreed, "and what is it that we believe about Jesus?" Here the group lapsed into what a former seminary professor used to call "the language of Zion" – churchy words that we've learned but would never use in an everyday context (students knew that using "the language of Zion" in a class sermon would get a thumbs down).

"Jesus died to save us from our sins," was the final answer. I pushed again: "Do you think that Buddhists and Muslims and people other religions will be condemned?"

"No!"

"Then why did Jesus have to die if everyone is going to be saved anyway ?"

More blank looks. Again, I'm not criticizing. I had not thought about this either until I realized the disconnect that exists between what we say in church and what we actually think about how God works in the world.

We are having an identity crisis. There are multiple reasons for it. One of them is the religious diversity in which we live. One option is to ignore it. Unfortunately, that has been the choice of many clergy and churches. But consider the growing number of intermarriages (in my youth, it was an identity crisis if a Lutheran married a Catholic!) and children are growing up with a wider knowledge of other religious traditions than ever before. What kind of support are we giving these families as they work through issues of their own identity?

From experience I know that interreligious pre-marital counseling is a different animal. Even when the couple professes to have no problems with each other's religion, issues do surface as we get further in-depth. One couple, a Lutheran and a Hindu, were surprised by my questions about the religious upbringing of future children. But they immediately realized that it was an important one. Two years later, when their son was born, we had a beautiful baptism that incorporated elements from both religions. Planning the ceremony was much easier because we had begun the conversation even before the wedding. Clergy and congregations must decide whether they will provide pastoral care to these families. And if they do decide to do that, will it be from a place of anxiety or from a place of openness?

Can we deal with our identity crisis in such a way that we are confident enough to welcome those with different identities without giving up our own?

Raimon Panikkar (1918 – 2010), Roman Catholic priest, professor and influential voice in interreligious dialogue was a child of a Hindu father and Catholic mother. He famously wrote, "I left Europe as a Christian, I discovered I was a Hindu and returned as a Buddhist without ever having ceased to be Christian."[54] As far back as 1976, he was addressing the question of Christian identity. In "Christian Identity in a Time of Pluralism," he puts it quite simply: "A Christian is someone for whom the word Christ discloses or illumines or touches, in one way or another, the central mystery of our existence."[55]

However, he also advises us that

> Christian identity is neither fixed once and for all, not left to the private interpretation of the individual. Christian identity consists rather in the dialogical interaction between a sincere confession and a collective recognition, each time according to a criteria considered valid at that particular juncture. It then falls

[54] Panikkar, Raimon , *Intrareligious Dialogue*. New York: Paulist Press, 1978, 2.
[55] Panikkar, Raimundo, "Christian Identity in a Time of Pluralism," *Pacific Coast Theological Society Papers 1939-1999*, Nov. 19-20, 1976, 27.

to the thinker to seek an underlying intelligibility in the series of statements affirming Christian identity.[56]

In other words, Christian identity must be reinterpreted thoughtfully and faithfully in every age. As challenging as this may be, sociologist Peter Berger has described our current theological scene as an unattractive choice between being wimps or thugs. He warns:

> To enter into such a dialogue is dangerous unless one has a very clear and confident idea of one's own experiences of truth. If one lacks such an idea, one will in short order be sucked into the worldview of whoever does have clarity and confidence. Therefore: No wimps! On the other hand, one cannot enter such a dialogue honestly (that is, without a covert missionary or pragmatically exploitative agenda) without accepting the risk that one's own position might change as a result of this encounter. Therefore: No thugs![57]

An example of this kind of well-differentiated identity is the (one would think unlikely) on-going dialogue between a Wiccan elder and a conservative evangelical Christian. Elder Don Frew of the Covenant of the Goddess and Brooks Alexander, one of the founders of the Spiritual Counterfeits Project, have developed a program called "Wiccan/Christian Dialogue: A 25-year Interfaith Friendship." [58] I can attest that these two interfaith pioneers are neither wimps nor thugs. They are secure in their own identities and are able to enter into areas of disagreement with grace.

So perhaps the better question would be: can we deal with our identity crisis in such a way that we become confident enough to enter into interreligious dialogue, knowing that it will be, as Berger describes "existentially risky, intellectually unpredictable, and

---

[56] Ibid, 26.

[57] Berger, Peter, *A Far Glory*. New York: Free Press, 1992, 77.

[58] Frew, Donald H. "When Wiccans & Evangelical Christians Become Friends." theinterfaithobserver.org. http://theinterfaithobserver.org/journal-articles/2012/1/11/when-wiccans-evangelical-christians-become-friends.html (accessed February 24, 2016).

sometimes socially awkward if not rude," yet also holding "the promise of new intuitions and insights?"[59] As you move through this book, it is my hope that your answer will be "Yes!"

FOR REFLECTION:

- What is your reaction to the story of removing the Paschal candle for the Jewish-Christian wedding?
- Do you agree that the Church is having an identity crisis? Why or why not?
- How would you answer (at least for today) the question: What does it mean to be a Christian?
- Are you or someone close to you in an interreligious marriage? Are you willing to share your experiences – both joys and challenges?

SUGGESTED READING:

- "From God's Perspective We Are All Minorities" by Krister Stendahl[60]

---

[59] Berger, Peter, 77.

[60] Stendahl, Krister. "From God's Perspective We Are All Minorities" sermonswithoutprejudice.org http://www.sermonswithoutprejudice.org/from-gods-perspective-we-are-all-minorities/ (accessed February 26, 2016).

PART II The Next Big Issue

"If Jesus were to come to earth now . . . Christ would introduce another revolution, another step, a new wine that he would not allow to be poured into old wine skins." – Raimon Panikkar[61]

Some years ago, a student from the Pacific Lutheran Seminary in Berkeley told me that, according to some of her professors, the interfaith Christology question is going to be the "next big issue" confronting the church. If this is so and if the theological and Christological task is to be more than an academic discussion among the clergy, seminary professors and other professional scholars, it is incumbent upon us to provide opportunities for people of faith to grapple with these issues respectfully and faithfully.

These next chapters will begin to lead us into an exploration of our theology and Christology. These are words that perhaps are intimidating to many lay readers. However, it is my hope that as we work through it together, we will help one another share stories about Jesus, thoughts about God, and begin to formulate a Christology for an interfaith world.

---

[61] Panikkar, Raimon, *The Intrareligious Dialogue*, 71.

Chapter 5   Doing Our Theology Together

Theology is "the pursuit of the heart of Being. - C.S. Song[62]

 While many in our churches today are attracted to interfaith events and courses on the world's religions, they may not be so excited about the idea of studying theology. As they strive toward becoming more inclusive and respectful in our diverse culture, they may not see any need at all to engage in any kind of theological quest. Theology is one of those words that can be intimidating to some and useless for others or it is seen strictly as the domain of the clergy. While I do believe that as a pastor I am called to be the "theologian in residence," I also firmly believe that all of us "do" theology, even if we're unaware that's what we're doing. Theology is simply God-talk; *theos* (God) and *logos* (word) – words about God. Of course it can – and does - get more complicated than that. However, that is no reason for any thinking person to consider herself or himself incapable of doing theology. In fact, they're probably already doing it.

 John Cobb defines theology simply as "intentional Christian thinking about important practical matters."[63] The fact is that Elsie was already struggling with her theology when she became concerned about "chasing after other gods." I believe that the multicultural and multifaith world in which we live today presents us with an imperative to do this kind of "intentional thinking." The matters before us are very practical. For instance, we can see our concerns about evangelism and declining church membership in a new light. How do we do evangelism if our purpose is not to convert? How do we reach out to those who are not able to make the exclusive claims of creeds and confessions? How do we incorporate their gifts into the lives of our congregations? In Cobb's words: "Unless the meaning of 'theology' is separated from its narrowing to academic theology and authoritarian pronouncements, the church is destined to continue to decay."[64]

 C.S. Song defines theology as "the pursuit of the heart of Being,"[65] In *The Believing Heart*, he extends an invitation to "thinking

---

[62] Song, Choan-Seng, *Doing Theology Today*. Madras: Christian Literature Society, 1976.

[63] Cobb, John, *Lay Theology*, St. Louis: Chalice Press, 1994), 12.

[64] Ibid, 82.

Christians to explore what Christian faith means in our life, and to think through how it relates to the world in which we live."[66] Like Diana Eck, Song describes a world that has changed:

> With the radical shifting of political, economic, and cultural dynamics, the religious dynamics have also shifted. The world of pluralism is here to stay. Christians cannot simply wish it away. The stakes for Christianity are indeed high if the Christian church ignores what religious and cultural pluralism means for human community, if it refuses to reinvision how God is at work on the world and in the whole universe.[67]

For Song it is the "believing heart" that informs our theology and is central to what he calls the "intense conversation" we have with the stories of our relationship with God. Telling stories is a way of doing theology that liberates and opens up a vast space of imagination and surprise.

> That vast space must be our theological space . . . It is the world of real people of flesh and blood, not the world of theological ideas and concepts. It is the world of tears and laughter, not the world developed by Christian minds and missionary enthusiasm. It is also the world in which men, women, and children commit sins and crimes against one another and in which they strive often in vain, but sometimes successfully, to reveal the divine light shining in the darkness of their hearts and in the depths of their community.[68]

With Cobb's "intentional thinking" and Song's "believing heart," we have a basis for doing the theology that is called for in our time. The same is true for our Christology – our words about Christ. Again, the subject can and does become complex. Yet every time I

---

[65] Song, Choan-Seng, *Doing Theology.*
[66] Song, Choan-Seng, *The Believing Heart: An Invitation to Story Theology.* Minneapolis: Fortress Press, 1999, 1.
67 Ibid, 4.
68 Ibid, 67.

think about Jesus - what I believe, how my beliefs relate to how I am in the world – I am doing Christology. And so are we all.

What I suggest, as we begin to delve into *inter*faith and *intra*faith matters, is that we do our theology and Christology together. I actually like the definition of theology given by C. S. Song better: "*theos* (God) and *logos* (discourse).[69] Since discourse is the use of words to exchange thoughts and ideas, that is dialogue, what better way to prepare for our interreligious conversations? Our *intra*faith explorations of our own faith tradition will serve us well as we dialogue with those of other belief systems. And our *inter*faith encounters will surely feed back into our internal discussions, creating a lively circle of God-talk. In the words of Professor Song, "Christian theology is strengthened and enhanced through the engagement with non-Christian religions."[70]

Granted, it might take some creative marketing to sell a theological quest to those who are as yet unaccustomed to thinking theologically or who are as yet unexposed to different concepts. But as Cobb writes, "theology is a responsibility of all Christians and that means primarily of lay Christians."[71] That does not mean that we all need to read heavy theological tomes. Through sharing stories and experiencing, thinking and reflecting we can embark on our theological quest together.

---

69 Ibid, 23.
[70] Ibid, 23.
[71] Cobb, *Lay Theology*, 72.

FOR REFLECTION:

- How do you feel about the statement "Theology is a responsibility of all Christians and that means primarily of lay Christians?"
- What do you think of the premise that not doing our theology is related to declining church membership?
- Why do you think some have said that the christological question is going to be the "next big issue" in our churches?
- Have you felt intimidated at the thought of doing theology? If so, do you feel less so now? How might you "sell" it to a reluctant church member?

SUGGESTED READING:

- *Lay Theology* by John Cobb[72]

---

[72] Ibid.

Chapter 6 We Begin with Jesus

The place of Christ in a multireligious society becomes an important issue in the search for a new theology of religions. — S. J. Samartha[73]

Back in the days of folk masses, when playing guitars in worship was radical business, there was a song called "He's Everything to Me."[74] I loved that song! Today I look at the title and wonder: who is the he; who is the me; and what is everything? The he, of course, is Jesus. The me is, well, me. And everything is the entirety of how I see the world, who I am in the world, and how I act in the world. There's more to it, of course. Everything includes a cosmos and a Divine Presence that permeates it all. Since I am part of creation, I exist within "Everything."

But I am not the same person I was in the 60s and 70s. Could it be that Jesus is not the same either? Was the author of the Letter to the Hebrews correct in proclaiming, "Jesus is the same yesterday, today and forever."?[75]

As I have listened to and read others' stories, experiences and understandings, I realize that my own understanding of Jesus has grown and developed. The "everything" I knew in my 20s is not the same I know today. So whether or not Christ is the same, I have changed. In the course of the story of my life, what I know of "everything" has expanded. Although I have also learned, as S. J. Samartha wrote:

> Jesus Christ is the same yesterday and today and tomorrow," but christologies need to change, redefine, and revise themselves constantly to make sense to the church and the world at different times and in different cultural situations. Such revisions have gone on at different times in the history of the church. They should be regarded as signs of vitality and the renewing power of the Christian faith in the world.[76]

---

[73] Samartha, S.J., *One Christ, Many Religions: Toward a Revised Christology*. Maryknoll, New York: Orbis Books, 1991, 76.

[74] Carmichael, Ralph, "He's Everything to Me," Communiqué Music/ASCAP, 1964.

[75] *The Inclusive Bible*, Hebrews 13:8.

[76] Samartha, S.J., 92.

When I became interested in the work of the Jesus Seminar and other scholars looking into the historic Jesus and the roots of Christianity, I had to take a new look at my own Christology. And when my autobiography began to include interreligious experiences, I was forced to really think seriously about who and what I mean when I say Jesus Christ.

My story is, by no means, unique. In a quick search of the library catalogue of the Graduate Theological Union in Berkeley, I found listings for LGBTQ, Latin American, African, feminist/womanist/mujerista and cosmic Christologies. Each of these disciplines has grown out of the stories of people who have followed Saint Anselm's definition of theology as "faith seeking understanding." They have applied their experiences as people of faith, seeking new understanding – in light of those life experiences.

There are also those scholars who have written – and continue to write – Christologies in light of interreligious encounters. S.J. Samartha's *One Christ, Many Religions: Toward a Revised Christology*[77] is but one of many such endeavors. However, this work should not be kept within the walls of academia. Each of us lives within a story; each of us makes meaning of the work and person of Jesus in light of our stories. As the author Frederick Buechner reminds us: "All theology, like all fiction, is at its heart autobiography."[78] Any desire to enter into interfaith dialogue as a Christian must take this into account.

A friend once described being in a program for training spiritual directors. Participants included Christians from around the world and from different denominations. She told the story of how they would sometimes get into theological and ecclesiological disagreements. Their solution: talk about their experiences of Jesus. The point was not to persuade others that their understanding was "correct" or to convert others to their way of theologizing their experience; it was simply to tell their stories.

This is similar to the advice offered by Benoit Standaert, a Benedictine monk from Belgium. In *Sharing Sacred Space*,[79] he suggests

---

[77] Ibid.

[78] Buechner, Frederick, *The Sacred Journey*. San Francisco : Harper & Row, c1982, 1.

[79] Standaert, Benoit, *Sharing Sacred Space: Interreligious Dialogue as Spiritual Encounter.*

the concept of "spiritual space." Starting from the recognition that "any encounter with the great religions of the world is doomed to fail if its starting point is dogma as formulated and transmitted in a given culture, or if it is based on some historical expressions, which are also culturally conditioned,"[80] Standaert suggests that we enter into interreligious dialogue from our "Jesus space."

As we prepare to enter into dialogue with people of other traditions, we must start with our own autobiographies, our own experiences and understandings of who and what Jesus Christ was and is. As we do so, we must also ask ourselves if we are open to considering other experiences and understandings. If we agree that " . . . although there is but one Jesus, there are several christologies within the New Testament,"[81] are we willing to go beyond our own stories and listen to the stories of others – within our own tradition? If we are willing, we will find a wealth of viewpoints, interpretation and ways of answering Jesus' question, "Who do you say that I am?"[82]

This issue often comes up for Christians who are invited to participate in interfaith services or to offer a blessing at an interfaith event. Unsure of how to express their Christian identity, many shy away from invoking the name of Jesus. To their credit, they are aware of how Christians have often overpowered such gatherings and do not want to be seen as continuing oppressive behaviors. I found myself in such a situation when I was asked to offer an invocation at a community interfaith event, along with a rabbi and an imam. As a pastor, I would represent Christianity - a daunting prospect in itself!

It was the first time I had been invited to do something like this and I had no idea how to represent Christianity in an inclusive, interfaith-friendly way. I ended up copping out. I chose a verse from the Hebrew Bible, Psalm 133: "See how good, how pleasant it is for God's people to live together as one!"[83] But I definitely felt outclassed! The rabbi blew the shofar and the imam chanted in Arabic. It all turned out well, however. As the three of us returned to our seats, with me in the middle, the iman reached out for my hand; I

Collegeville, MN: Liturgical Press, 2009.
[80] Ibid, viii.
[81] Samartha, S.J., 112.
[82] *The Inclusive Bible*. Matthew 16.15, Mark 8.29, Luke 9.20.
[83] *The Inclusive Bible*. Psalm 133:1.

took the rabbi's hand with my other hand and drew it across to the imam's. As I looked down at our hands, now all three joined together, I knew this kind of space was where I wanted to be. I also began to learn that clear self-definition did not have to mean exclusivism. The next time I spoke at an interfaith gathering, I spoke from my tradition, using the words of Jesus.

If indeed we are in the midst of a new reformation within Christianity – and I believe we are – then it is certainly incumbent on clergy and laity alike to enter into the theological spirit. The best way to begin would be to tell our own stories about Jesus to one another.

During Lent one year, we used the *Saving Jesus* series, a DVD curriculum from a progressive Christian standpoint (from the folks at *Living the Questions*).[84] After we showed the segment entitled "What Can We Know About Jesus (and How)?" one of the participants asked, "Why aren't we hearing this stuff from the pulpit?!" My response was one that I have often heard from speakers (some of whom were featured on the DVD). They agree on the fact that not everyone will be at the same place in their readiness to hear different ideas about core religious beliefs. Their advice is to not preach these from the pulpit, but instead introduce them in an adult forum series where there is openness to discussion and acceptance of where individual members are. In other words, they encourage us to do our theology together.

We will go further into theology and Christology in later chapters, as well as how to create a safe environment for participants of differing opinions.

---

[84] http://www.livingthequestions.com

FOR REFLECTION:

- Do you have a favorite story from the gospels about Jesus?
- Can you think of a story that Do you have a favorite picture of Jesus in your mind (from a painting, illustration or sculpture)?
- someone else has told you about Jesus?
- Has your knowledge/understanding of Jesus changed at all at any point in your life?

SUGGESTED READING:

- The Gospel According to Mark

Chapter 7   God-Talk

I would argue that if Christian theology has nothing to say about the vast world of millions of people with vibrant, diverse, passionately held religious beliefs and practices, it is hardly living up to its name as "God-talk.[85]

- Kristin Johnston Largen

Changing slightly the title of a recent book by Rob Bell,[86] let me ask this question: what *do* we talk about when we talk about God? I would guess that most Christians have some idea in mind when they say "God." I would also guess that not all of those concepts would be the same.

For our mid-week Lenten series several years ago, we read *Speaking Christian* by Marcus Borg[87]. The week we discussed the chapter on God, I put two columns on a sheet of newsprint. One column was "Being;" the other "Sacred Presence" (Borg's categories). According to Borg, the first refers to a being beyond and separate from the universe. The second does not refer to a being separate from the universe, but to a sacred presence all around us. I asked the members of our discussion group to think of words or names which had the most meaning for them in reference to God. We quickly filled both columns.

Since the group was comprised of members of several different congregations, we had a good variety of answers. The "Being" column was filled with personified names for God, such as Father, Mother, Lord, Yahweh and Ruler of the Universe. The "Sacred Presence" column was filled with phrases such as Ground of Being, Holy One, Divine Presence and Source of All Being.

It was fun and enlightening to hear one another's stories of why these designations were meaningful and to understand that what is valuable for one might, in fact, be difficult for another. As we enter into dialogue with other religions, a conversation like this one can be an important part of the foundation on which we stand.

---

[85] Largen, Kristin Johnston, *Finding God Among Our Neighbors: An Interfaith Systematic Theology.* Fortress Press, 2013, 7.

[86] Bell, Rob, *What We Talk About When We Talk About God.* New York, NY: HarperOne; Reprint edition, 2014.

[87] Borg, Marcus, *Speaking Christian.* New York : HarperCollins, 2011.

So, what do *you* talk about when you talk about God? Most people assume that all Christians are theists. Theism (sometimes referred to as "classical theism" or "supernatural theism") is belief in one God who transcends the world, yet is also immanent in it. While both transcendence and immanence are understood as part of God's nature, it often seems as though many people believe that God is very far   away, looking down on them. A member of a congregation I once served described his concept of God. He said that in order to keep tabs on every person on earth, God had to be sitting at a bank of computer screens which constantly scanned the world. The song "From a Distance" illustrates this perfectly. The lyrics tell us:

> God is watching us
> God is watching us
> God is watching us, from a distance.[88]

This heavy emphasis on transcendence leads me to a brief sidebar about deism. Best known as the faith of some of our Founding Fathers, such as Thomas Paine, Benjamin Franklin, and Thomas Jefferson, deism also emphasizes a God who is transcendent but not immanent. But, unlike the God who is "up there" watching us, the God of the deists is often likened to a divine watchmaker, who created and wound up the world, and then let it run by itself. A quote often attributed to Thomas Paine claims, "God exists, and there it lies."[89]

Deism was a product of the Enlightenment, when activities previously understood as the work of God could now be explained by science. Philosophers of the day posited, therefore, that God, though the creator of the world, was now totally removed from it. I mention this because of deism's birth in the wake of scientific discoveries.

---

[88] Gold, Julie, "From a Distance," Nanci Griffith, MCA Records, 1987.

[89] There is no "source" for this. It's a paraphrase of several articles by Paine. It's been around so long that it's taken as a factual quote by Paine. If he indeed said this as it's written I've never seen it and I've read, I believe, every work of Thomas Paine that I'm aware of. In fact Paine often says "God does not exist" We must understand that the quote is a summation of all of Paine's works. - Dr. Ben Johnson, Doctor of Divinity, Deist.

While it may not be a theology we hear much about today, science is still having a great impact on how we understand God.

Getting back to theism, I have to now return to the story from Chapter 3 about atheists, in which Marcus Borg asks his students to describe the God they don't believe in. He says, "Invariably, it is the God of supernatural theism. They're simply not aware that there is an option other than supernatural theism. That option is, of course, panentheism."[90]

Let me be perfectly clear here. Borg is not talking about pantheism. Pantheism ("all is God) is the belief that God is synonymous with the universe, not separate from but totally identified with the world. According to pantheism "God is everything and everything is God," in other words, *all* immanence.

In contrast, pan*en*theism ("all-in-God") is a way of conceptualizing God, not as a supernatural being, separate from Creation, but as a Presence all around us. "God is more than the universe, yet the universe is in God."[91] Theologian Sallie McFague suggests that we see "the world as the body of God."[92]

This is not a new concept. Both supernatural theism and panentheism can be found in the Bible, however, classical Christianity has emphasized one over the other. A good example of panentheism in the New Testament is the statement in Acts attributed to Paul that God is "the One in whom we live and move and have our being."[93]

Borg offers a way for us to conceptualize this idea. In *The God We Never Knew*, he writes:

> I sometimes seek to explain the difference between panentheism and supernatural theism by inviting my students to imagine how one might diagram God in relation to the universe. I suggest representing the universe with an oval. Where is God in relation to the universe? Supernatural theism thinks of God as being outside of the oval; God and the

[90] Borg, Marcus, The Heart of Christianity: Rediscovering a Life of Faith. New York: HarperCollins, 2003, 69.
[91] Borg, Marcus, The God We Never Knew. San Francisco, CA: HarperSanFrancisco, c1997.12
[92] McFague, Sallie, Models of God: Theology for an Ecological, Nuclear Age. Minneapolis, MN: Fortress Press, 1993, 60.
[93] The Inclusive Bible, Acts 17:28.

universe are spacially separate. Panentheism would represent God as a larger oval that includes the oval of the universe; God encompasses the universe, and the universe is in God. Of course, these diagrams cannot be taken literally. It does not make sense to think of either the universe or God as having borders, as the ovals suggest.[94]

While panentheism may not be a household word to many people, it is present in a number of familiar religious groups. Many Native American religions are panentheistic. Creation Spirituality, popularized by Matthew Fox's *The Coming of the Cosmic Christ* [95] and *Original Blessing*,[96] and Process Theology have panentheistic components. Panentheism also appears in mystical traditions of Judaism, Islam, as well as Christianity. It is also expressed in the *Bhagavad Gita* of Hinduism.

In Buddhism, the Reverend Zen Master Soyen Shaku wrote a series of essays collected into the book *Zen For Americans*. In the essay titled "The God Conception of Buddhism" he attempts to explain how a Buddhist looks at the ultimate without an anthropomorphic God figure while still being able to relate to the term God in a Buddhist sense:

> At the outset, let me state that Buddhism is not atheistic as the term is ordinarily understood. It has certainly a God, the highest reality and truth, through which and in which this universe exists. However, the followers of Buddhism usually avoid the term God, for it savors so much of Christianity, whose spirit is not always exactly in accord with the Buddhist interpretation of religious experience. To define more exactly the Buddhist notion of the highest being, it may be convenient to borrow the term very happily

---

[94] Borg, *The God We Never Knew.*

[95] Fox, Matthew, *The Coming of the Cosmic Christ: the healing of Mother Earth and the birth of a global renaissance.* San Francisco: Harper & Row, 1988.

[96] Fox, Matthew, *Original Blessing.* Santa Fe, N.M.: Bear, 1983.

coined by a modern German scholar, "panentheism," according to which God is πᾶν καὶ ἕν (all and one) and more than the totality of existence.[97]

There are many ways of talking about God. As we move into talking with those with ways different from our own, it would be well for us each to identify and share our ways of conceptualizing the Divine. This *intra*faith exchange of ideas among ourselves will give us a deep well from which to draw as we enter into our *inter*faith conversations.

FOR REFLECTION:

- Do you conceptualize God more as "Being" or "Sacred Presence?"
- What names, if any, do you like to use for God?
- How do you experience God's transcendence? Immanence?

SUGGESTED READING:

- *What We Talk About When We Talk About God* by Rob Bell[98]

---

[97] Shaku, Soyen, *Zen for Americans*. Translated by Daisetz Teitaro Suzuki. La Salle, Ill., Open Court [1974, c1906].
[98] Bell.

Chapter 8   "Who Do You Say I Am?"

. . .issues of Christology cannot be avoided in an interreligious conversation that professes to take Christian faith claims seriously. – Kristin Johnston Largen[99]

Is a professed belief in Jesus Christ the only way to salvation? When Rob Bell published his book, *Love Wins: A Book About Heaven, Hell, and the Fate of Every Person Who Ever Lived,*[100] in 2011, his answer in essence was "No." Accusations of heresy immediately began to fly from Bell's evangelical community. Bell anticipated their criticism in the book:

> As soon as the door is opened to Muslims, Hindus, Buddhists, and Baptists from Cleveland, many Christians become very uneasy, saying that then Jesus doesn't matter anymore, the cross is irrelevant, it doesn't matter what you believe, and so forth. Not true. Absolutely, unequivocally, unalterably not true.[101]

Whether or not you agree with all of Rob Bell's conclusions, he has certainly highlighted the challenge for Christians today as we come into contact with those of other religious traditions (as well as many within our own).

There are a variety of ways we can address this challenge. Kristin Johnson Largen, associate professor of systematic theology at the Lutheran Theological Seminary at Gettysburg, offers several ways we could deal with this question of salvation. We could, as many do, limit it to those who profess Christ as the one who brings salvation. If we choose that option, the conversation, in terms of developing an interfaith-friendly Christology, is over. As the bumper sticker proclaims: "God said it, I believe it and that settles it!"

---

[99] Largen, 137.
[100] Bell, Rob, *Love Wins: A Book About Heaven, Hell, and the Fate of Every Person Who Ever Lived.* New York, NY: HarperOne, 2011.
[101] Ibid, 155.

Or we could take a more expansive view. If we do that, then there are, according to Largen, at least two further options. One is Christian universalism, the belief that all people will be saved through Christ whether or not they professed faith in Christ in their lives. And although this position has always been controversial (just ask Rob Bell!), there is support from early church teachers, such as Origen, Clement of Alexandria and Gregory of Nyssa, and more contemporary ones, such as J. A. T. Robinson and William Barclay. These and other Christian thinkers provide one model of answering the question before us.

The second way Largen describes is perhaps not as familiar, although it corresponds to the concept of Pluriform Pluralism (more about that in Chapter 11). This is "the idea that there is more than one positive ending to a life of faith, whether that is the paradise described in the Qur'an or the enlightenment described in the Heart Sutra."[102]

But before we become entangled in these different propositions, it would be good for readers to reflect for a moment on their own current Christology. Again, the word may be intimidating, but it's really very simple. The term "Christology" simply means what or who you think Christ is, and what exactly is the relationship of Christ to Jesus. That may seem like a moot question since the official councils and creeds of the early church established the "orthodox" teachings with which we are familiar.

However, when we read the gospels, we find the basis for differing ways of answering the question. One way of getting at this is to ask whether you have a high Christology or a low one. Both are found in the New Testament. Mark, the earliest gospel, has the lowest Christology. John, written last, has the highest. Biblically speaking, the further away you get from the actual time of Jesus' life on earth, the higher the Christology. Putting it very simply, a low Christology, such as Mark's, emphasizes the human aspects of Jesus. A high Christology, such as found in John, emphasizes Jesus' divinity, identifying him as the Logos, present with God at the beginning of time and one with God.

---

[102] Largen, 142.

Another way of looking at is in terms of doing Christology from above (high) or from below (low). A Christology from above begins with the divine nature of Christ and then moves to the incarnation ("In the beginning was the Word and the Word was made flesh.") The emphasis is on the Christ of faith, the post-resurrection Jesus, on whom the early church based its doctrines and creeds. This is the Christology of the Nicene Creed, which many today are questioning as the only way of understanding Christ.

Christology from below, on the other hand, begins with the historical Jesus. For many, it has been important to reclaim the importance of the human life and teachings of Jesus and to then move toward understanding the Divine nature. This is the starting point for the many liberation theologies (e.g. feminist, queer, black, womanist), which build upon the contexts of the human condition from a particular perspective.

Then we have those theologians who encourage us, as we encounter other religions, to adopt a theocentric Christology. This means that, rather than affirming Jesus as the final, definitive and universally normative revelation of God (Christocentric Christology), we would move to one that "stresses the universal revealing activity of God and confesses Jesus as a universally relevant but not necessarily definitive and normative expression of that revelation."[103]

S. J. Samratha (1920-2001), Indian theologian and first director of the World Council of Church's "Dialogue with People of Living Faiths and Ideologies" subunit, would be such a proponent. In *One Christ – Many Religions: Toward a Revised Christology,*[104] he suggests that we adopt a "theocentric (or Mystery centered) Christology." He defines Mystery as "the transcendent Center that always remains beyond and greater than apprehensions of it, or even greater than the sum total of those apprehensions."[105] In this way we are free to talk theologically with those of other religious traditions. It does not mean, however, that we diminish the centrality of Jesus Christ in

---

[103] Knitter, Paul. "Theocentric Christology" academiccommons.columbia.edu. http://academiccommons.columbia.edu/catalog/ac%3A146170 (accessed February 26, 2016).

[104] Samartha, S.J., *One Christ – Many Religions: Toward a Revised Christology.* Maryknoll, New York: Orbis Books, 1991.

[105] Ibid, 82-83.

Christian faith:

> If, according to the earliest tradition of the New
> Testament, Jesus Christ always pointed to God and is
> therefore himself theocentric or God centered, then the
> only way to be Christ centered is to be God centered,
> but in a religiously plural world, being Christ centered is
> not the only way to be God centered.[106]

On the other hand, C. S. Song, professor emeritus of
Theology and Asian Cultures at the Pacific School of Religions,
worries that "by getting rid of Christocentrism, one may at the same
time be getting rid of Jesus."[107] While he admits to and agrees with
many of the problems of a Christ-centered faith, which he believes is
often really a church-centered faith and theology in disguise, he
advocates, not for a theocentric faith, but for one that is Jesus-
oriented.

But perhaps the question we really should be asking first is:
what are we talking about when we say *salvation*? The answer may
seem obvious: salvation is our deliverance from sin and its
consequences through the death and resurrection of Jesus Christ, i.e.,
our ticket into heaven. But a study of the hundreds of times that
salvation and words from the same root will reveal that there are many
other ways that the word is used.

In *Speaking Christian: Why Christian Words Have Lost Their
Meaning and Power - and How They Can Be Restored*,[108] Marcus Borg lists
some of these: for example, salvation as liberation from bondage, as
return from exile and as rescue from peril. He also includes the
communal aspect, such as moving from injustice to justice and from
violence to peace. In the end, Borg's definition of salvation is not only
personal but also communal: "the twofold transformation of
ourselves and the world."[109]

---

[106] Ibid, 93.
[107] Song, Choan-Seng, *The Believing Heart*, 62-3.
[108] Borg, Marcus, *Speaking Christian: Why Christian Words Have Lost Their Meaning and
Power - and How They Can Be Restored*. New York: HarperCollins, 2011.
[109] Ibid, 54.

But he understands that this is not the common useage. In fact, he puts *salvation* at the top of his list of words to be restored. In the chapter entitled "Salvation," he describes an intergenerational discussion group he once facilitated. Most of the participants were Christians who were actively involved in their churches. The rest of the group was made up of those who had never been or were no longer part of a church, but were still drawn to Christianity. Borg relates:

> For 80 percent of the group, *salvation* had *only* negative associations. These went back to childhood and teenage years. Salvation was about going to heaven. Though that might sound appealing, the opposite possibility – going to hell - was deeply alarming. Salvation as "going to heaven" affected their understanding of its sibling terms *saved* and *savior*. Because the obstacle to going to heaven was sin, to be *saved* meant being saved from their sins. *Savior* referred to Jesus dying for their sins in order to make their salvation possible. They recalled, even as children, worrying about whether they had believed and behaved as they needed in order to be saved. Salvation was laden with anxiety, subsumed as it was within a fear-based Christianity. Many of these left the church, often for decades; resentment and rejection replaced fear.
>
> Most also reported being bothered by the exclusiveness that went with this understanding of salvation. They were told, or absorbed, that only Christians could be saved – that is, go to heaven. Salvation was associated with a sharp division between those who were saved, who were "in," and those who were not.[110]

Borg has identified the *intra*faith difficulties of both our language and our doctrines. Within Christianity, the "language of Zion" needs to be redeemed. In fact, Borg was going to call his book *Redeeming Christian Language* until he realized *redeeming* was one of the

---

[110] Ibid, 36-37.

words that need to be redeemed! In defining *salvation* as "the twofold transformation of ourselves and the world, " he concludes that "This is what Christianity at its best is all about. And this is what the religions of the world at their best are about."[111] If, as Christians, we are willing to take an expansively biblcal view of salvation, we may have less difficulty with including those of other belief systems.

These issues will reappear later on the book. The point, for now, is to begin to challenge yourself to articulate your own answer to Jesus' question: "Who do you say I am?" There is no need to be discouraged if some of these concepts are confusing or your Christology does not come to you in a neatly wrapped package tied with ribbon. Our journey has just begun and we will continue to explore together.

FOR REFLECTION:

- How have you understood who or what Christ is?
- Would you describe your Christology as high (from above) or low (from below)?
- What is your reaction to some theologians' proposal that we move to a theocentric Christology?
- What is your definition of salvation? Has this been a positive or negative association for you?

SUGGESTED READING:

- *Speaking Christian* Marcus Borg[112]

---

[111] Ibid, 54.
[112] Borg, *Speaking Christian.*

PART III Faces of God

It turns out that there is a clear disconnect between how the media and academics identify American believers and how they identity themselves. - Baylor Institute for Studies of Religion

People are the heart of this work. We have to start with people where they are. In working with congregational members on *inter*faith and *intra*faith matters, there are no simple, one-size-fits-all answers. It is important to create trusting personal relationships in which questions can be taken seriously, without fear of condemnation.

As we enter into area that will perhaps be more challenging for some, I will begin with a plea for going beyond mere tolerance for people of other religions. Then I will begin to help readers locate themselves and others in the *intra*faith landscape, introducing them to classical positions of exclusivism and inclusivism. Finally, before we move into the complexities of pluralism, I will pause for an examination of some of the fears that arise when entering the *inter*faith scene, specifically accusations of heresy, syncretism and relativism.

Chapter 9   Beyond Tolerance

Tolerance ... usually has an elitist lining; either an elitist lining in the sense that you can be tolerant because for you it is not that important, or an elitist lining of noblesse oblige ‑ I know, but I cannot expect the other to know as much as I do.
– Krister Stendahl[113]

Words matter. The meanings of words also change. Consider the ongoing discussions about the differences between interfaith and multifaith or between interfaith and interreligious. That debate is a topic for another book, but it points to the evolving picture of this work.

We could say the same of the word "tolerance." I've often seen the "Practice Tolerance" bumper sticker, with "Tolerance" spelled out with symbols of the world's religions, and know that it's meant to be an inclusive sentiment. When Swami Vivekananda addressed the World Congress of Religions in Chicago in 1893, he spoke of "a religion which will have no place for persecution or intolerance in its polity."[114] Since the Congress was the first formal gathering of representatives from both Eastern and Western traditions, it is easy to understand why he paired persecution and intolerance in his speech. Tolerance was then a great improvement over prejudicial beliefs and actions.

But there are problems with the word tolerance. It can imply a willingness to put up with something disagreeable or disliked. If I say that I tolerate you, I convey a very different thing than if I say that I admire or respect you. The issue came to the fore in the global arena in the year 2000 at the United Nation's Millennium Religion Summit. As reported by Rajiv Malhotra, founder of the Infinity Foundation[115], Swami Dayananda Saraswati, the head of the Hindu delegation

---

[113] Stendahl, Krister, "From God's Perspective We Are All Minorities," from a lecture delivered on February 27, 1992, at the Center for the Study of World Religions, Harvard University, as edited by Arvind Sharma and Jennifer Baichwal

[114] Vivekananda, Swami. "The World's Congress of Religions, The Addresses and Papers Delivered Before the Parliament." parliamentofreligions.org https://www.parliamentofreligions.org/sites/default/files/Vivekananda.pdf (accessed February, 2016).

[115] The Infinity Foundation (http://infinityfoundation.com) is a non-profit organization based in Princeton, New Jersey. Part of their mission is to promote East-West dialogue.

proposed that the term "mutual respect" be substituted for the word "tolerance" in the Summit's final document "Commitment to Global Peace."[116] According to Malhotra, the words became a fierce topic of debate, in which adherents of the Abrahamic religions were strongly challenged to respect the non-Abrahamic religions as equals. Mere tolerance was not enough.

This was not a matter of mere political correctness. Christians, by agreeing to go beyond tolerance to mutual respect, begin to swim into the deep waters of church teachings about salvation. Although Cardinal Joseph Ratzinger (the future Pope Benedict), head of the Vatican delegation, objected strongly to the wording of the resolution, "mutual respect" won the day. However, the Vatican quickly issued a statement that affirmed that while "followers of other religions can receive
divine grace, it is also certain that objectively speaking they are in a *gravely deficient situation* in comparison with those who, in the Church, have the fullness of the means of salvation." [117]

Inherent in these challenges is the Christological question: in light of our religious diversity who and what is Jesus? If we do not reject the truth claims of other traditions, we may have some problems with our own. These dilemmas are not solely academic exercises. They are very practical issues that need to be addressed, for example, in our practices of evangelism and mission. As Asian theologian C. S. Song has written: "The problem of Christian mission is the problem of Christian theology. Reconstruction of Christian theology must then precede reconstruction of Christian mission."[118]

It is not merely a matter of political correctness at the congregational level either. The question of tolerance or respect may relate to our willingness to be open to the real people we meet in

---

[116] "Whereas there can be no real peace until all groups and communities acknowledge the cultural and religious diversity of the human family in a spirit of mutual respect and understanding" (from *Commitment to Global Peace*, The Millennium World Peace Summit of Religious and Spiritual Leaders, Millennium World Peace Summit)

[117] Congregation for the Doctrine of the Faith. "Dominus Iesus: On The Unicity And Salvific Universality of Jesus Christ and the Church." vatican. http://www.vatican.va/roman_curia/congregations/cfaith/documents/rc_con_cfaith_doc_20000806_dominus-iesus_en.html (accessed February, 2016).

[118] Song, Choan-Seng. "What Is Christian Mission?: Starting Again with Jesus " (paper distributed in a class at the Pacific School of Religion).

interfaith encounters, to engage in dialogue which goes beyond tolerance. As Swami Dayananda and Cardinal Ratzinger found, however, moving from tolerance to mutual respect is not without challenges.

In another workshop I led at an interfaith gathering, the group consisted of Christians of different denominations, with one exception: Don, a Wiccan elder. As I usually do, I had people pair up and share their stories and then report back to the group. Don had been partnered with a Lutheran pastor from the more conservative Missouri Synod.[119] As Don reports, "We were sitting together on a small couch and when some discussion turned to accepting diversity, he said something about how could be pleasant with all sorts of non-Christian folks "... like Don, here [putting his arm around my shoulders], who is going to Hell" [with a big smile]. I think he genuinely thought he was being accepting." This pastor was very clear that while he liked Don personally and enjoyed their conversation, he could not accept Don's religious views. Someone in the group asked him whether he believed that if Don did not accept Jesus as his savior, he would not be saved. He answered in the affirmative. The other Christians in the group were appalled and looked to me to (I assumed) correct him. The calmest person in the room, though, was Don, who was quite used to being told by Christians that he was going to hell. And since he doesn't believe in hell or the need for a personal savior, he is able to enter into interfaith dialogue without anxiety.

To me, this incident did not reveal bigotry on this pastor's part. He was simply stating what his church teaches. He was perfectly able to tolerate the faith beliefs of others, but he could not move into mutual respect. And if they are honest, many people in our congregations will be in the same place. When we try to move beyond tolerance, we run into our own beliefs and the church teachings we have accepted as normative for a long, long time.

In my own work on interfaith councils, I have found this to be true for myself as well. I discovered that I had a line (sometimes

---

[119] The Lutheran Church Missouri Synod (LC-MS) is a Lutheran denomination, not to be confused with the Evangelical Lutheran Church in America (ELCA). More conservative in its theology and biblical interpretation, LC-MS disagrees with the ELCA on many issues, including ecumenical partnerships and the ordination of women and practicing LGBTQ candidates.

conscious, sometimes not) that I could not cross. I could accept some religions as valid, but others were much more problematic. Tolerance was not an issue; that was easy. But respect was something else. For example, the interfaith scene in the Bay area includes a number of people from the Bay Area Family Church, part of the Family Federation for World Peace and Unification (commonly called the Unification Church), founded by Rev. Sun Myung Moon. I know several members of the church from interfaith events. I even gave a talk at one of their meetings.

The problem for me came when one of these interfaith friends invited me to a banquet honoring Rev. and Mrs. Moon when they visited San Francisco in 2005. While I felt honored to be invited, I also had some trepidation as I entered the ballroom of the Hilton Hotel. I met up with Jan and Paul Chaffee from the Interfaith Center at the Presidio[120] and we sat together through a church ritual, the dinner and a very long speech by Rev. Moon.

Actually, we left before the speech was over because it had gotten so late. As we walked out of the hotel, we discussed what we had experienced. We agreed that there were some aspects of the evening that had been challenging for us. We discussed what we would say to our friends who had invited us that would be appreciative of them, yet honest about our differences in theology.

Later, as I reflected on the evening, I tried to be more objective. I had to admit that there are rituals in other traditions that I do not like or from which I am excluded, others teachings with which I disagree. There are also leaders in other traditions I find problematic. I certainly do not agree with every belief statement of every religious group (even within Christianity!). So what would cause me to draw the line at this one?

I know people who balk at the inclusion of the Pagan community. Others struggle with the Mormons. Other interfaith activists have a hard time accepting newer religions, such as Religious Science, Unity or Sufism Reoriented. It seems we each have a line between tolerance and respect that we cannot cross. I have

---

[120] The Interfaith Center at the Presidio, according to its web site "is a San Francisco Bay Area grassroots interfaith friendship-building nonprofit organization, welcoming people of all faiths at the Interfaith Chapel in the Presidio of San Francisco (the Presidio Chapel), an interreligious advocate of peacemaking among religions, locally and globally."

discovered, however, that when I listen and learn about the "other," my line shifts. I cannot say that it has been obliterated, but I also cannot dismiss a group out of hand without a serious inquiry into my own motivations, prejudices and blind spots.

Moving from tolerance to mutual respect is a serious undertaking. It means that we have to venture out of our Christian bubble. As a result of the growth of diversity in the American population, we now have the task of rethinking who and what we are. As we listen and learn about what others believe, we are confronted with an increasing need to re-articulate our own faith identity. As we look at similarities and differences among religions, we are finding the need to look more closely at our own doctrines, biblical interpretations and worship practices. The question that arises is: are other religious paths equally valid, and if they are, then what does it mean to be a Christian?

Not everyone will want to venture into this kind of exploration. I have found a number of Christian responses to religious diversity. Some retreat into the sanctity of their own traditions and simply reject any and all claims of truth from other religions. Others drift into relativism and simply state that "it's all the same God anyway, so it really doesn't matter."[121] A third response is to refuse to deal with these questions at all. It is not my goal to criticize any of these, especially the third. A lot of good interfaith cooperation happens without delving into theological inquiries.

But it is my contention that, as leaders in the Christian church, we need to move into both *inter*faith and *intra*faith engagement. If we accept the challenge to move beyond tolerance to mutual respect, the *intra*faith encounter may be our most provocative one of all.

---

[121] In no way are these responses limited to Christianity. Other traditions must also struggle with challenges to their belief systems. However, as a Christian pastor, it is my intention to address these issues within the context of the Christian community.

FOR REFLECTION:

- How do you define tolerance? Mutual respect?
- Can you understand Swami Dayananda's side of the argument? Cardinal Ratzinger's?
  How did you react to the story of Don and the Lutheran pastor?
- What would you have said to them?
- Are there religious groups you find you cannot tolerate? Respect?
- Have you ever experienced intolerance of your beliefs?
- Where is your line? Has it ever moved?

SUGGESTED READING:

- *Beyond Tolerance: Searching for Interfaith Understanding in America* by Gustav Niebuhr[122]

---

[122] Niebuhr, Gustav, *Beyond Tolerance: Searching for Interfaith Understanding in America.* New York: Viking, 2008.

Chapter 10   Perspectives: Exclusivism and Inclusivism

First and foremost, the central theological issue of religious pluralism is the Christological one, "Who do you say that I am?" - David S. Nah[123]

While we may all acknowledge the diversity of our current culture and even the reforming movement happening in the church, we will find ourselves all over the map in how we think about other religions. The three general categories are: exclusivism, inclusivism and pluralism. In this chapter I will describe the characteristics of the classic positions of exclusivism and inclusivism, with the caveat that there are many different ways of defining these words.

Exclusivism

Exclusivism is the claim that Jesus Christ is the only way to salvation; if Jesus died for the sins of the world, then no other way of salvation is needed. Exclusivists claim that salvation is given only to those who make an explicit commitment to Jesus Christ; other religions are erroneous. Scripture passages such as "I am the way, the truth, and the life, no one comes to the Father but by me"[124] and "There is no salvation in anyone else, for there is no other name under heaven given to the human race by which we must be saved"[125] are taken absolutely literally. There are, however, variations all along the exclusivist spectrum. At the far extreme are those with a narrow interpretation of scripture; the theological lines are drawn sharply and inflexibly. But there are many exclusivists, such as the Lutheran pastor in Chapter 9, who are more open to wrestling with the issues raised by encounters with other religions. Charles Kimball reminds us:

> Many Christians who would categorize themselves as exclusivists point to the Book of Job and Paul's Epistle to the Romans as they readily concede that no one knows the mind of God. They are committed to

---

[123] Nah, David S., *A Critical Evaluation Of John Hick's Theology Of Religious Pluralism.* A Dissertation submitted to the Faculty of Claremont Graduate University in partial fulfillment of the requirements for the degree of Doctor of Philosophy in the Graduate Faculty of Religion, Claremont, California 2005.
[124] *New Revised Standard Version*, John 14:6.
[125] *The Inclusive Bible.* Acts 4:12.

bearing witness to the revelation of God in Jesus Christ even as they openly advocate tolerance and respectful dialogue and practice cooperation across religious lines. Since public attention most often gravitates toward people with the most extreme views, it is important to recognize that one can embrace an exclusivist theology and also interact productively with people in other traditions.[126]

A primary representative of the classical exclusive position is the Dutch Missionary, Hendrik Kraemer (1888–1965). His position is clearly stated in his major work, *The Christian Message in a Non-Christian World*: "God has revealed *the* Way and *the* Life and *the* Truth in Jesus Christ and wills this to be known through all the world."[127] The purpose of mission is to "persuade the non-Christian world to surrender to Christ as the sole Lord of Life"[128] and therefore should not be abandoned in the Christian encounter with other religions. For Kraemer, an exclusive position did not preclude practical cooperation (in medical, educational, and social services), religious tolerance, and willingness to learn from non-Christian religions. Not all exclusivists would agree. Illustrating the differences within these positions is Kraemery's belief that knowledge and experience of other religions were necessary, as opposed to Karl Barth who, when asked how he knew that Hinduism was unbelief when he had never met a Hindu, replied, "a priori."[129] Barth asserts the supremacy of the Christian faith as simply obedience to the truth which has been revealed in Jesus Christ.

The value of an exclusive position is its certainty. As Raimundo Panikkar writes,

This attitude has a certain element of heroism in it. You consecrate your life and dedicate your entire existence to something which is really worthy of being

---

[126] Kimball, Charles, *When Religion Becomes Evil*. NY: Harper Collins, 2002, 203.

[127] Kraemer, Hendrik, *The Christian Message in a Non-Christian World*. New York: Harper and Row, 1938, 107.

[128] Ibid, 8.

[129] Niles, Daniel, "Karl Barth – A Personal Memory," *The South East Asian Journal of Theology* (1969): 10-11, quoted in D'Costa, 54.

called a human cause, to something that claims to be not just a partial and imperfect truth, but a universal and even absolute truth.[130]

From the point of view of interfaith dialogue, however, there are problems with this viewpoint, the first being the obvious danger of intolerance. Another problem is language, especially words such as salvation and sin. For example, sin as the basic human problem, is a distinctly western perception. In some Eastern religions it is suffering, not sin, that is the basic condition from which we need release. In many instances there is a breakdown in communication because of the language we use (a "comparing apples and oranges" effect). To scholars of other religions "salvation, defined as a category that denotes a person's ultimate destination in heaven or hell, looks like a very Christian concern or even obsession."[131]

Inclusivism

Inclusivism is an attempt to mediate between exclusivism and pluralism. Its roots can be traced back to John Farquhar (1861-1929), a Scottish Protestant missionary in India. In *The Crown of Hinduism*,[132] Farquhar posited that it is Christ, not Christianity, that is the fulfillment of Hinduism and missionary activity should not destroy, but rather fulfill, Hinduism's potential: Christ provides the fulfillment of the very highest aspirations of Hinduism . . . In Him is focused every ray of light that shines in Hinduism. He is the Crown of the Faith of India.[133]

Inclusivism is exemplified by Roman Catholic theologian Karl Rahner (1904–1984). Rahner accepts the pluralists' argument that an all-loving God could not condemn the majority of humankind

[130] Panikkar, Raimundo, *The Intrareligious Dialogue*. New York: Paulist Press, 1999, xv.

[131] Forward, Martin, *Inter-religious Dialogue: A Short Introduction*. Oxford: Oneworld, 2001, 44.

[132] Farquhar, John, *The Crown of Hinduism*. London; New York: Humphrey Milford; Oxford University Press, 1915.

[133] Race, Alan, *Christians and Religious Pluralism: Patterns in the Christian Theology of Religions*. London: SCM Press, 1983, 57.

because they are not Christians. But he also agrees with the exclusivists that salvation comes only through faith in God through Christ. In order to reconcile these seemingly contradictory beliefs, Rahner proposed that it is possible for God to be present and to bring about salvation through non-Christian religions. This does not negate the claims of Christianity because the presence of God in these other religions is, in fact, the presence of Christ, and adherents might be known as "anonymous Christians."[134] Mission is still important because the proclamation of the gospel turns an anonymous Christian "into someone who also knows about his Christian beliefs in the depths of his grace-endowed being by objective reflection and in the profession of faith which is given social form in the Church."[135]

In 1964, the Second Vatican Council adopted a text called "Lumen Gentium" (Light to the Gentiles), which says that:

> those, who through no fault of their own do not know Christ or his Church, but who nevertheless seek God with a sincere heart, and moved by grace, try in their actions to do his will as they know it through the dictates of their conscience – those too may achieve eternal salvation.[136]

More recent is the 2013 homily by Pope Francis, in which he declared: "The Lord has redeemed all of us, all of us, with the Blood of Christ: all of us, not just Catholics. Everyone! 'Father, the atheists?' Even the atheists. Everyone!"[137]

The value of the inclusive perspective is that it believes that with Christ as the one supreme savior of the world, salvation is at

---

[134] Ariarajah, S. Wesley, *The Bible and People of Other Faiths*. Geneva: World Council of Churches, 1985, 10.

[135] Rahner, Karl, *Theological Investigations, vol. 5*. Baltimore: Helicon Press, 1966), 132, quoted in Gavin D'Costa, *Theology and Religious Pluralism: The Challenge of Other Religions*. Oxford: Basil Blackwell, 1986), 88.

[136] Flannery, Austin P., ed., *Documents of Vatican II, 2nd ed.* Grand Rapids, MI: Eerdmans, 1980, 367, quoted in Charles Kimball, *When Religion Becomes Evil.* NY: Harper Collins, 2002, 203.

[137] Catholic Online (NEWS CONSORTIUM). "Pope Francis says atheists can do good and go to heaven too!" catholic.org. http://www.catholic.org/news/hf/faith/story.php?id=51077 (accessed February 26, 2016).

work throughout the world, whether others know it or not. This comes as a great relief to many people who want to hold to the exclusive claims of Christianity, while at the same time allowing for the inclusion of others. This would be the position of Rob Bell and other Christian universalists from Chapter 8.

The problem with this perspective from the point of view of other religions, as well as that of many Christians, is that their differences from Christianity are downplayed. Other religions are seen through Christian lenses and measured by Christian standards. Affirmation of the other religion is contingent on making it compatible with Christianity. At a meeting of the World Council of Churches in 1971, Metropolitan Georges Khodr exemplified this position: "Christ is hidden everywhere in the mystery of his lowliness. Any reading of religions is a reading of Christ. It is Christ alone who is received as light when grace visits a Brahmin, a Buddhist or a Muhammadan reading his own scriptures."[138]

It has been argued that the concept of the anonymous Christian is offensive to non-Christians, in that it reflects chauvinism and paternalism and is an "honorary status granted unilaterally to people who have not expressed any desire for it."[139] It also creates a stalemate in dialogue, since "it is just as easy, and as arbitrary, to label devout Christians as anonymous Muslims, or anonymous Hindus, as to label devout Hindus or Muslims as anonymous Christians."[140]

And again we have the problem of language. Words like sin, salvation, redemption, repentance, even faith are not found in some other religions. Even while trying to be inclusive, the assumption of agreement on the spiritual problems of all people may be seen as presumptuous.

These two perspectives, exclusivism and inclusivism, are places where many people in our congregations will be located. While it may be comfortable to remain with just these two, we will now begin to go deeper.

---

[138] Cited in Race, Alan, *Christians and Religious Pluralism: Patterns in the Christian Theology of Religions.* London: SCM Press, 1983, 50.
[139] Hick, John, *God Has Many Names.* Philadelphia : Westminster Press, c1982, 68.
[140] Ibid.

FOR REFLECTION:

- Do you find yourself drawn to either exclusivism or inclusivism?
- Is either of these positions the way you have understood Christianity?
- Is there any difference in how you think about Christian belief and how you feel?
- Where in the worship services you've attended have you observed either of these positions?

SUGGESTED READING:

- *Christians and Religious Pluralism: Patterns in the Christian Theology of Religions* by Alan Race
    - Chapter 2 "Exclusivism"[141]
    - Chapter 3 "Inclusivism"[142]

---

[141] Race.
[142] Ibid.

Chapter 11   Heresy, Syncretism and Relativism – Oh, My!

Do you suppose we'll meet any wild animals? – Dorothy in The Wizard of Oz

When one begins to become involved in interfaith exploration, it is common to hear dire warnings against becoming a heretic, a syncretist or a relativist – or all three! Before we launch into a survey of pluralism, I believe it would be wise to take some time to look at these supposed pitfalls in order to 1) understand what they are, 2) defang these "wild animals" so they're not so frightening, and 3) become competent in explaining them to others.

Heresy

Heresy is another word for freedom of thought. - Graham Greene

Years ago, when I was planning a synod-wide worship service, my bishop requested a preview of the bulletin. His first comment, "You can't say that; it's a heresy" caught me completely off-guard. First of all, I didn't know which heresy I had stumbled into. When I asked, he told me that my attempts to use inclusive language for the Trinity was modalism. I had to wait until later to look it up; I guess my Church History classes on heresies hadn't sunk in very well.

Back then I was intimidated by such an accusation. The line between orthodoxy and heresy was clear; one did not cross that line or question it. However, I knew that there were differing ideas about just who was a heretic and who wasn't. In my first year of Lutheran seminary I was talking to my neighbor, who was attending a nearby Bible college. She excitedly told me that in the current semester they were studying cults. "I had no idea," she exclaimed, "that the Catholic Church is a cult!!" At the time I was amused, thinking that I knew who the "real" heretics were. Years later, though, her words came back to me. When questions about whether Mormonism was really Christian or a cult came up in the 2012 presidential election, I wondered who gets to say who is and who isn't a "real" Christian.

My willingness to ask this question does not mean an "anything goes" acceptance of every religious claim that comes down the pike. Living in San Francisco, which still has memories of people lost in Jim Jones' People's Temple, has taught me that the danger of cults is real. But as Bart Ehrman reminds us in *Lost Christianities: The Battles for Scripture and the Faiths We Never Knew*,[143]

> among the many expressions of Christianity that existed in the years before the biblical canon was formed and a standardized belief system put in place, even the apostle Paul was considered a heretic by at least one group of believers.[144]

A thorough exploration of the classic heresies is not the purpose of this book. What I hope is that readers will be brave enough to think and discuss their beliefs without fear of the Inquisition coming to burn them at the proverbial stake.

As S. J. Samartha advises:

> In raising serious and critical questions about traditional christologies handed over to Asian Christians by the west, and in calling for a revision of inherited christologies, one risks the danger of being accused of heresy. This risk has to be taken for the sake of Jesus Christ, even if it might mean a rejection by one's friends and colleagues.[145]

And finally, at the risk of ignoring my own advice to abstain from pointing the finger at possible heretics, I conclude with words of wisdom from Jesuit priest and theologian, Karl Rahner, who said:

> If you are talking about God and you're talking about anything that has to do with God (whether it's ritual or sacraments or scriptures or morality or anything) and you are sure you know what you are talking about, you are a heretic.[146]

---

[143] Ehrman, Bart, *Lost Christianities: The Battles for Scripture and the Faiths We Never Knew*. New York: OxfordUniversity Press, 2003.

[144] The Ebionites held that following the laws of the Old Testament was necessary for salvation. Paul, with his teaching of justification by faith in Christ apart from works of the law, was dismissed as a heretic.

[145] Samartha, S.J., *One Christ, Many Religions: Toward a Revised Christology*. Maryknoll, New York: Orbis Books, 1991, 119-120.

Quoted by Megan McKenna in "Painting the Stars, Session 7: An Evolving

I take these words, not as an accusation against anyone, but as a reminder to myself to keep an open mind.

Syncretism
No religious revolution...is possible without paying the price of syncretism.

-Carsten Colpe (1929-2009) German scholar of religion, New Testament scholar and Iranist

A few yeas ago, my congregation participated in an initiative called *Faith Shared: Uniting in Prayer and Understanding* sponsored by the Interfaith Alliance[147] and Human Rights First.[148] The project, in which Christian churches across the country hosted readings from the Qur'an, was part of an act of solidarity with the Muslim community to send a message both here at home and to the Arab and Muslim world about our respect for Islam. I was astonished by the flurry of negative emails and comments on our church's web site. Several quoted the Bible to defend their messages. For example:

> Your (*sic*) planning to send "a message both here at home and to the Arab and Muslim world about our respect for Islam" with a time to read the Quran during worship this Sunday. Second Corinthians 6:14-18 says we're forbidden to do that kind of thing. It's one thing to be friendly with someone in Islam, but it's a whole

---

Spirituality: Mysticism." DVD.
http://www.livingthequestions.com/xcart/home.php?cat=485 (accessed February 26, 2016).

[147] The Interfaith Alliance celebrates religious freedom by championing individual rights, promoting policies that protect both religion and democracy, and uniting diverse voices to challenge extremism. http://interfaithalliance.org

[148] Human Rights First is an independent advocacy and action organization that challenges America to live up to its ideals. "We believe American leadership is essential in the global struggle for human rights, so we press the U.S. government and private companies to respect human rights and the rule of law. When they fail, we step in to demand reform, accountability and justice. Around the world, we work where we can best harness American influence to secure core freedoms." http://humanrightsfirst.org

other thing in a Christian community to be reading something that is antithetical to Christianity and is hostile to Jesus Christ himself. You should be ashamed of yourself and resign never to preach in a Lutheran or Christian church again.

Several accused us of becoming "Chrislam," a hybrid of Christianity and Islam. That was a new one to me! The accusation was really that we are syncretists.

Syncretism, the fusion of different forms of belief or practice, is feared by many as destructive to their own religious traditions. They believe that it is essential to preserve the purity of the religion and its doctrines and practices. Therefore speakers, readings or prayers from another religion are not acceptable. Whether or not one holds a pluralistic position, it should be recognized, however, that syncretism was a part of the creation of most present-day religions.

For instance, despite Old Testament diatribes against the indigenous religions of Canaan, scholars have documented their effects on the evolution of Judaism. Later Judaism would incorporate contributions from Zoroastrianism, such as the identification of Satan as the Evil One and the angelology found in the book of Daniel. The idea of an afterlife in a heaven or a fiery hell can also be traced to Persian roots:

> Judaism also began to develop its own theology of heaven and hell after its contact with Zoroastrianism. The pre-exilic Biblical books do not make reference to "afterlife." The early Israelite theology was simply that. We came from dust and would return to dust. With the

first exile and the new immense exposure to the religion of the Persian Empire, Zoroastrianism, the "Jewish" afterlife stories become mainstream.[149]

Of course, Christianity, which already has its own roots in Judaism, inherited those Zoroastrian characteristics. As Lawrence Heyworth Mills (1837 – 1918), Professor of the Persian language at Oxford University summed it up: "It pleased the Divine Power to reveal some of the most important articles of our Catholic creed first to the Zoroastrians, and through their literature to the Jews and ourselves."[150]

As the new religion spread out into the Greco-Roman world, it also came into contact with the Hellenistic Mystery Religions, in which participation was restricted to those initiated into secret ritual and practices. In a paper written while a student at Crozer Theological Seminary in 1949-50, Martin Luther King concluded: "There can hardly be any doubt of the fact that these ceremonies and beliefs strongly coloured the interpretation placed by the first Christians upon the life and death of the historic Jesus."[151]

The most obvious influence on Christianity was Greek philosophy. There can be no doubt that the concept of the "logos" of the Gospel of John comes from the "logos" of Heraclitus, the pre-Socratic philosopher. And the language of "substance" the Nicene Creed, establishing the doctrine of the Trinity, has its origins in Aristotilian philosophy.

---

[149] Hurvitz, Mitchell M. "Syncretism and the Zoroastrian influence on Judaism." greenwichtime.com.
http://www.greenwichtime.com/opinion/article/Syncretism-and-the-Zoroastrian-influence-on-4732682.php (accessed February 24, 2016).

[150] Gier, N F. "Religious Syncretism." webpages.uidaho.edu.
http://www.webpages.uidaho.edu/ngier/syncretism.htm (accessed March 3, 2016).

[151] King, Martin Luther. "The Influence of the Mystery Religions on Christianity." kinginstitute.stanford.edu.
http://mlkkpp01.stanford.edu/index.php/kingpapers/article/volume_i_29_november_1949_to_15_february_1950g/ (accessed February 24, 2016).

This can certainly be seen in Asian Christianity. In my own studies, it has been scholars such as C.S. Song from Taiwan, Fumitaka Matsuoka from Japan and Paul Chung from Korea who have opened my eyes to other paradigms and possibilities. They taught me that I cannot forget that the lenses through which I look are thoroughly Western. In contrast to Western thought with our doctrines and creeds, the Asian Christian way of viewing Ultimate Reality is more perceptual and intuitive. It is also able to be more open and inclusive, perhaps because of the fact that it has had to co-exist as a minority along with other religions such as Islam, Buddhism and Hinduism. Because of this, Asian Christians may be able to teach Christians in the West about discussing syncretism openly and faithfully in a world of religious diversity.

All of these examples illustrate what Nicholas F. Gier, Emeritus Professor of Philosophy at the University of Idaho called the "Number One Principle of Comparative Religion: the Principle of Religious Syncretism." This principle holds that when any two cultures meet and interact they will exchange religious ideas with the dominant culture prevailing in the exchange. [152]

I would, however, challenge the second half of Gier's principle - that the dominant culture will prevail. Today, in our supposedly dominantly Christian nation, many people are incorporating aspects of other religions into their own. This could mean either 1) Gier's principle is flawed or 2) Christianity is no longer the dominant religion. But the first part of the principle is certainly as true today as it was in ancient times: when any two cultures meet and interact they will exchange religious ideas. However, this does not mean that we engage in what Alan Race calls "an easy syncretism."[153] His suggestion for a truly pluralistic theology is that we hold the different types of religious experience together in a creative tension.

---

[152] Gier, N F. "Religious Syncretism." webpages.uidaho.edu. http://www.webpages.uidaho.edu/ngier/syncretism.htm (accessed March 3, 2016).
[153] Race, 104.

I do believe that it is necessary to interject here a word of caution about appropriation, that is, borrowing from other cultural and religious traditions. Again, this is not a clear-cut issue. One Sunday, some of our seminary students (who are required to undergo sensitivity training for this) objected to our use of a Native American prayer. They raised a good question and I pursued input from other clergy, both white and Native American. The responses I got were inconclusive. Most thought that there was nothing wrong with using the prayer as long as attribution was given. Some asked how it was different from singing Negro spirituals or hymns from Africa and Latin America. I realized that we have a long way to go in overcoming our propensity to "borrow" things to which we have no right. My intention here is simply to raise awareness of this as we think about incorporating the religious practices of others into our own.

Relativism
Through the incarnation in Jesus Christ, God relativized himself in history.
– S. J. Samartha[154]

Most of the time, when you come across the word "relativism," it is preceded by "the danger of." Even though we know quite well that everything is relative, our knowledge is limited and we are products of our environment; when it comes to interfaith relationships, "relativism" is a pejorative term.

Relativism holds that ethical truths depend on the individuals and groups holding them, and that therefore all views are equally valid. However when it comes to interfaith theology, Alan Race warns:

> the apparent danger of pluralism in the Christian theology of religions is that if all religions are made relative it could undermine concern to distinguish good from bad, the spiritually wholesome and profound from the spiritually poor and moribund religions. It could imply the first steps toward an undifferentiated syncretism and that choice between

---

[154] Samartha, S.J., 76.

the traditions would be rendered arbitrary or meaningless.[155]

For some "undifferentiated syncretism" might not seem like such a bad idea. To be honest, it is the position of many liberal Christians, whose response to awareness of religious diversity is to state, "we're all talking about the same thing." However, Geoffrey Parrinder points out that this position is "unsatisfactory if it is taken to mean that all religions are the same, which they clearly are not, or that it does not matter what people believe. Questions of truth and goodness are important. The religion of the ancient Aztecs, who held up the beating hearts of their victims to the sun, was clearly not so good a faith as the peaceful way of the Buddha."[156]

This is not only a Christian challenge. At an interfaith retreat I co-led, I attempted to broach the subject of how we deal with our differences and was met with resistance. One man (in what I thought was a condescending attitude) "explained" that there was no need for such a discussion, that we were "all on the same page here." Later, however, in two separate incidents, the issue of Islam's teaching about homosexuality became divisive. One woman actually left the retreat. Those who remained were then willing to have the conversation after all.

There are differences among the religions, as well as similarities. And here is where we run into the challenge to Christians who want to be accepting of other spiritual paths, yet know that there are aspects of our scripture and doctrines that would preclude us from doing so. There seems to be no middle ground between absolutism and relativism. Yet today's theologians are taking up the challenge. As we work through our own theologies, we would be wise to heed the words of Alan Race, who advises: "The pertinent question mark which hovers over all theories of pluralism is how far they succeed in overcoming the sense of debilitating relativism, which is their apparent danger."[157]

---

[155]Race, 78.

[156] Parrinder, Geoffrey, *Encountering World's Religions*. Edinburgh: T & T Clark, 1987, 224, quoted in Martin Forward, *Inter-religious Dialogue: A Short Introduction*. Oxford: Oneworld, 2001, 41.

[157] Race, 90.

The key word here is "debilitating," which is not a descriptor any of us would want. So how are we to navigate between what Leonard Swidler calls the "absolutist view of the truth of the meaning of things . . ." and "the silence of total relativism"?[158] If we are serious about doing our theology faithfully, we will undertake the challenge of walking the line between these two extremes.

The first step of the process is admitting that each of us has a standpoint that has been conditioned by a multitude of factors. Therefore, we must be diligent about digging diligently to identify our own pre-suppositions. Even among Christians of a particular denomination or congregation, no discussion should begin with "Of course we all believe that . . ." (even in churches that confess a creed each Sunday). Do these presuppositions mean that we are relativists? Well, yes. Even theologian John Cobb, who has also expressed concern about "debilitating relativism," puts it bluntly:

> Perhaps relativism should simply be affirmed. Indeed, I have often called myself a relativist. I have often understood relativism to be the affirmation that every event, every assertion, every belief is conditioned by a multitude of factors: physical, social, historical, psychological, biographical, and so forth. This is almost self-evidently true. For me this is good news. It can free us *from* the question of certainty and *for* a far less inhibited, more imaginative search for insight and understanding. In this sense I enthusiastically endorse relativism.[159]

However, before we dismiss Cobb as a heretic, be assured that he then qualifies his position and warns: "Taken to its most consistent and extreme limit, it (relativism) leads to solipsism."[160] He navigates

---

[158] Swidler, Leonard, "The Age of Global Dialogue," *Marburg Journal of Religion*: Volume 1, No. 2 (July 1996), 15-16.

[159] Cobb, John, "Responses to Relativism: Common Ground, Deconstruction and Reconstruction," *Soundings* 73.4 (Winter 1990), 595-6.

[160] Solipsism is a theory holding that the self can know nothing but its own modifications and that the self is the only existent thing; also : extreme egocentrism. *Merriam-Webster Dictionary*, s.v. "solipsism," accessed February 26, 2016, http://www.merriam-webster.com/dictionary/solipsism.

the path by stating: "Relativism in this sense is compatible with strong convictions while encouraging the hope for the attainment of more nearly adequate ways of thinking."[161]

Which brings us to the second step of the process: dialogue with those of other standpoints. As Leonard Swidler wisely advises:

> . . . we need to engage in dialogue with those who have differing cultural, philosophical, social, religious viewpoints so as to strive toward an ever fuller perception of the truth of the meaning of things. If we do not engage in such dialogue we will not only be trapped within the perspective of our own "standpoint," but we will now also be aware of our lack. We will no longer with integrity be able to remain deliberately turned in on ourselves. Our search for the truth of the meaning of things makes it a necessity for us as human beings to engage in dialogue. Knowingly to refuse dialogue today would be an act of fundamental human irresponsibility -- in Judeo-Christian-Muslim terms, a sin.[162]

Perhaps Maurice Friedman can be of help here. He suggests that a "dialogue of touchstones" (or ultimate concerns) is the answer to the either/or of an exclusivist absolutism and a hopeless relativism.[163] His approach is about persons and groups, rather than official religious bodies. It allows room for a wide variety of positions, but without any need to convince or convert. What I like about Freidman's proposition is the presupposition that those engaging in such a dialogue will have come in with a clear idea of their own touchstones. The process of coming up with those offerings is one from which each of us can benefit.

Finally, Peter Berger assuages our fears:

[161]Ibid, 615.

[162]Swidler, Leonard, "The Age of Global Dialogue," *Marburg Journal of Religion*: Volume 1, No. 2 (July 1996), 15-16.

[163]Friedman, Maurice, "The Dialogue of Touchstones as an Approach to Interreligious Dialogue," in Gort, Jerald, et al, eds. *Dialogue and Syncretism: An Interdisciplinary Approach*. Grand Rapids: W.B. Eerdmans, 1989.

It is largely because of my conviction that such a contestation between the faith held by the Church and other faiths is actually possible and potentially fruitful that I am not finally troubled by the impact of cultural pluralism. The pluralizing forces of modernity do indeed relativize all belief systems, but the truth will come out again and again. Truth resists relativization.[164]

As you can see, all three of these subjects raise serious question and are worthy of our attention. However, using them as a means of deeming some thoughts and ideas off limits or as threats to open and honest conversation would be detrimental to our *intra*faith process.

FOR REFLECTION:

- Has anyone ever called you a heretic, a syncretist or a relativist?
- Would you describe yourself with any of these terms?
- Have you ever used these terms to describe someone else?
- How do you feel about Judaism and Christianity being the product of syncretism?
- How might the issues and questions raised in this chapter be of use to you in interfaith relationships?

SUGGESTED READING:

- *Lost Christianities: The Battles for Scripture and the Faiths We Never Knew* by Bart Ehrman[165]

---

[164] Berger, Peter, *A Far Glory: the quest for faith in an age of credulity*. New York: Free Press, 1992, 77.

[165] Ehrman, Bart, *Lost Christianities: The Battles for Scripture and the Faiths We Never Knew*. New York: Oxford University Press, 2003.

PART IV Pluralism

I believe that it is impossible to be a faithful and relevant Christian today without coming to terms with the realities of religious pluralism. - Bruce Epperly[166]

Now we enter into a subject much more difficult to categorize than exclusivism and inclusivism. While those categories also have their sub-groupings, pluralism is an ever-expanding field with a plethora of titles, subtitles and explanations.

So let me be clear: this brief survey is in no way exhaustive. In fact, as more is continually written on the subject, it is hard to keep up! Also, I do not intend this book to be an in-depth theological text; my goal is to help pastors and congregations *do* theology. In the past fifteen years, as I have been wrestling with these questions, I have come to understand that the quest for a pluralistic theology is an ongoing process. There is no definitive answer. But if we can accept that it is a process, we can enter into it with a spirit of openness and adventure.

What I hope to accomplish in these chapters is to offer a smorgasbord of ideas, hopefully whet the reader's appetite to take a taste of something perhaps strange and new.

---

[166] Epperly, Bruce. "The Adventurous Lectionary: Epiphany Sunday. patheos.com. http://www.patheos.com/blogs/livingaholyadventure/2012/12/the-adventurous-lectionary-epiphany-sunday (accessed February 26, 2016).

Chapter 12 Venturing into Pluralism

We have no good reason to believe that any one of the great religious traditions has shown itself to be more productive of love/compassion than another.

– John Hick[167]

Now, as we move beyond the exclusive and inclusive view that God's revelation in Jesus Christ is unique and normative, we find a complex array of options. As we begin to make our way into this labyrinth, we must first understand that pluralism is another one of those words that can have a variety of meanings. The first year that my congregation observed Pluralism Sunday,[168] a member emailed to ask exactly what "pluralism" was. Depending on my answer, he wasn't sure he could support it. I appreciated his question because the word is thrown around a lot; you will often see it used interchangeably with diversity, interfaith and multiculturalism.

But as a theological position, it is much more specific. A pluralist affirms other religions as authentic ways of salvation or liberation on their own terms. Claims of Christianity as either the only way (exclusivism) or the hidden fulfillment of other ways (inclusivism) are rejected. So, for instance, when you go to the Pluralism Sunday web site,[169] you see under the heading *Pluralism Sunday: Celebrating the Many Paths to God*:

> Progressive Christians thank God for religious diversity! *We don't claim that our religion is superior to all others. We recognize that other religions can be as good for others as ours is for us.* (italics mine) We can grow closer to God and deeper in compassion—and we can understand our own traditions better—through a more intimate awareness of the world's religions.[170]

---

[167] Hick, John, *The Metaphor of God Incarnate: Christology in a pluralistic age.* Louisville, KY: Westminster John Knox Press, 2006, 138.

[168] Pluralism Sunday was first sponsored by the Center for Progressive Christianity (now ProgressiveChristianity.org) on Pentecost 2007. Since then, it's observed on the first Sunday in May.

[169] http://pluralismsunday.org.

[170] Ibid.

Although the last decade of the 20th century brought about a flurry of writing about pluralism, the position is not new. It can be traced back to Ernst Troeltsch (1865-1923) in his essay "The Place of Christianity among the World's Religions"[171] and William Hocking (1873–1966) in *Rethinking Missions*.[172] Both argued that Christianity could not claim any special status among the world's religions; it was one among many equally valid paths to salvation. This shift in thinking challenged the claim that Christ was the only revelation of God. Troeltsch, for instance, acknowledged the experience of God through Christ, but countered with the qualification that "this experience is undoubtedly the criterion of its validity, but be it noted, only of its validity *for us*."[173]

I observed an illustration of Troelsch's quote in the adult forum of a Lutheran church. I had invited Paul and Jan Chaffee from the Interfaith Center at the Presidio in San Francisco to meet with the group. The people who attended were open and were mostly interested in interfaith cooperation, not so much in theological quandaries. One member who had been raised by parents in the mission field abroad was especially enthralled with Paul, who is also the child of missionaries. While strongly identified as a Christian, she also had an open mind to the challenges that other faiths bring us.

After the meeting, a young man approached and explained that he hadn't been able to attend the forum because he taught a Sunday school class, but he had a question. It was the usual "What about Jesus as the Way, the Truth and The Life?" The response of Jan Chaffee was classic Troelsch: "Jesus is the Way for Christians, not for everyone." The best way to describe what happened next is in the words of Matthew 19:22: "When the young man heard this, he went away sad." I realized then how difficult the answer is for members of congregations who are asking the question in all seriousness, yet perhaps not yet ready to embrace a pluralistic view.

---

[171] Troeltsch, Ernst , "The Place of Christianity Among the World Religions" in *Christian Thought: Its History and Application,* edited by Baron von Hügel. NY: Meridian Books, 1957, 35-63.

[172] Hocking, William, *Rethinking Missions,* New York and London, Harper & Brothers, 1932.

[173] Troeltsch, 26.

Here we arrive at the heart of the dilemma of religious pluralism: what about Jesus? Getting serious about pluralism means accepting a profound challenge to the core Christian belief that Jesus is the unique Son of God and the only savior of humanity. And here we must tread very lightly. While some will be excited by new ways of thinking about core Christian beliefs, others will be very threatened. In a beginning discussion group, it will be enough for participants to be open to hearing about differing ways of understanding, with no expectation that everyone accept them. In fact, we should remind ourselves that there are even many different varieties of pluralism; even pluralists are not all in agreement! As Roman Catholic theologian Paul Knitter says: "To expect a unified response among New Testament scholars on the question of Jesus' uniqueness would be about as naïve as to look for a consensus on economic theory among Washington politicians."[174]   As we explore the various ideas being put forth by Christian scholars wrestling with these questions, we can see how *intra*faith is just as necessary as *inter*faith dialogue.

A good place to begin an exploration of pluralism is with the work of Diana Eck, arguably the most familiar pluralist today. She has become well known through her work on the Pluralism Project at Harvard University and books such as *The New Religious America*[175] and *Encountering God: a Spiritual Journey from Bozeman to Benares.*[176] Her description of pluralism is "the engagement of our differences in the creation of a common society.[177]   On the Pluralism Project web site, rather than offering a more concise definition, she give us "four points to begin our thinking."

In the first point she clarifies the distinction between diversity and pluralism: "Pluralism is not diversity alone, but *the energetic engagement with diversity.*"[178]

---

[174] Knitter, Paul *No Other Name? A Critical Survey of Christian Attitudes toward the Worlds Religions.* Maryknoll, NY: Orbis Books, 1985, 173.

[175] Eck, Diana, *The New Religious America How a "Christian Country" Has Become the World's Most Religiously Diverse Nation.* San Francisco: HarperSanFrancisco, 2001.

[176] Eck, Diana, *Encountering God: a spiritual journey from Bozeman to Banaras.* Boston: Beacon Press, 1993.

[177] Eck, Diana. "Our Religion, Our Neighbors, Ourselves." PBS.org. http://www.pbs.org/wgbh/pages/frontline/shows/faith/neighbors/ (accessed February 24, 2016).

The second point addresses the limitations of religious tolerance: "Pluralism is not just tolerance, but *the active seeking of understanding across lines of difference.*"[179]

The third point begins to get at the often-expressed fear that pluralists are on a slippery slope of relativism: "Pluralism is not relativism, but *the encounter of commitments.* The new paradigm of pluralism . . . means holding our deepest differences, even our religious differences, not in isolation, but in relationship to one another."[180]

Finally, Eck's fourth point gives us the methodology of pluralism: "Pluralism is *based on dialogue.* The language of pluralism is that of dialogue and encounter, give and take, criticism and self-criticism. Dialogue means both speaking and listening, and that process reveals both common understandings and real differences. Dialogue does not mean everyone at the "table" will agree with one another. Pluralism involves the commitment to being at the table -- with one's commitments."[181]

These points give us a way to begin our thinking, however they do not answer all our questions. Nor do they try; Eck is not offering a pluralist theology or Christology. Is such a thing even possible? That question was once posed to Welton Gaddy, former executive director of the Interfaith Alliance in Washington, D.C.[182] His response was that he thought that it is not. His advice to those who would enter into interreligious encounters was to listen to one another.[183] While his view, seen from the perspective of a political organization, is understandable, many are making the attempt to make theological

---

[178] Eck, Diana, "What is Pluralism?" pluralism.org. http://www.pluralism.org/pluralism/what_is_pluralism (accessed February 26, 2016).

[179] Ibid.

[180] Ibid.

[181] Ibid.

[182] The Interfaith Alliance, 1331 H Street, NW, Washington, DC 20005, was founded in 1994 to promote interfaith cooperation around shared religious values to strengthen the public's commitment to the American values of civic participation, freedom of religion, diversity, and civility in public discourse and to encourage the active involvement of people of faith in the nation's political life.

[183] Gaddy, Welton, "A Strategy for Interfaith Cooperation and Understanding," (lecture presented at the Chautauqua Institution, June 27, 2001),Chautauqua, NY.

sense of our multi-religious world. Ever since the days of Troeltsch and Hocking, other theologians have been busy grappling with the question of how to be faithful to Jesus while also opening up to others for whom Jesus is not "the Way."

And now the subject gets very complicated. Different branches spring (and continue to spring) from the pluralism tree. I could attempt to distill the thinking of theologians on the subject, but that would take a whole other book, and frankly others have already done that. My intention is to give you a taste of where scholarship is today – with the caveat that it is a work in process; scholars themselves are creating a river that is flowing and alive with life. For those who want definitive answers, this concept may seem like their worst nightmare. But if we step into the river without fear, with openness to learning about other ways of answering our deepest questions, perhaps we will discover some answers for ourselves.

REFLECTION QUESTIONS

- What is your "gut reaction" to the statement from the Pluralism Sunday web site: "We don't claim that our religion is superior to all others. We recognize that other religions can be as good for others as ours is for us."?
- How do you think it could be possible to "grow closer to God and deeper in compassion -and we can understand our own traditions better - through a more intimate awareness of the world's religions"?
- How might Diana Eck's "four points to begin our thinking" help us in our *inter*faith and *intra*faith conversations?
- What do you think she means by the encounter of commitments?

SUGGESTED READING:

- *The Divine Deli* by John H. Berthrong[184]

---

[184] Berthrong, John H., *The Divine Deli: Religious Identity in the North American Mosaic.* Maryknoll, NY: Orbis Books, 1999.

Chapter 13   Pluralism 101

We have barely begun to deal with the fundamental changes that must be effected within our Christian faith. – John Cobb[185]

So here we go! Understand that this is by no means the only way that pluralist theologies are categorized. Different authors use different names and classify theologians differently.[186] Since the subject – and the theologians themselves - are ever-evolving, making a definitive statement is like trying to nail Jello to a wall. But one of the simplest syntheses comes from Gavin D'Costa, who lists the shared characteristics of all pluralists:[187]

- Christ is one revelation among other equally important revelations.
- Religions can learn about the divine from each other.
- The days of religious imperialism and chauvinism are over.
- Mission is understood as dialogue.

He also provides a nice and simple breakdown of three kinds of pluralists: unitary, pluriform and ethical. I will describe each one briefly and then go into further detail about them.

---

[185] Cobb, John, in Griffin, David Ray, ed., *Deep Religious Pluralism*. Louisville, KY: Westminster John Knox Press, 2005, 65

[186] Anselm Min in "Dialectical Pluralism" uses these classifications: ". . . there are the phenomenalist pluralism of John Hick and Paul Knitter that takes religions as diverse phenomenal responses to what is ultimately the same ineffable transcendent reality, and the universalist pluralism of Leonard Swidler, Wilfred Cantwell Smith, Ninian Smart, Keith Ward, and David Krieger that stresses the possibility and necessity of a universal theology based on insights from the history of religions. Rosemary Ruether, Marjorie Suchocki, Tom Driver, and Paul Knitter propose an ethical or soteriocentric pluralism that insists on justice as a measure of all religions (Hick and Knitter), while Raimundo Panikkar advocates an ontological pluralism that asserts the pluralism not only of our knowledge of being but of being itself (Swidler 1987; Hick and Knitter). There is, finally, the confessional pluralism of Hans Küng (Swidler 1987), John Cobb (Swidler 1987; D'Costa), Jürgen Moltmann, J.A. DiNoia, John Milbank, Kenneth Surin (D'Costa), and Mark Heim that insists on the legitimacy and necessity of each religion to confess itself precisely in its particularity including the claim to finality."[186]

[187] D'Costa, Gavin, *Christianity and the World Religions: Disputed Questions in the Theology of Religions*. Oxford: Blackwell, 2009, 7.

Unitary pluralists are proponents of the "different paths up the same mountain" belief that there is a single (unitary) divine reality behind all religious expressions. All religions are oriented toward the same religious goal, whether we use names such as "God," "Ground of Our Being," or "Nirvana" and each leads to the same end. Each religion, therefore, is a valid and equal path.

Pluriform pluralists, on the other hand, believe that religions can be on different paths, moving towards different summits. They would have us understand that different religions promote different ends and that for the sake of integrity we should recognize the differences in the beliefs, practices, and hopes among us. As David Ray Griffin explains:

> "Religious diversity involves real differences in the diagnosis of the basic human problem, the type of "salvation" needed, and the nature of the ultimate reality to which attention is directed." [188]

Finally, ethical pluralists do not want to judge religions by their concepts of divine reality at all. They believe that religions are related to the Divine insofar as they hold to ethical beliefs and practices.

---

[188] Griffin, David Ray, ed., *Deep Religious Pluralism*. Louisville, KY: Westminster John Knox Press, 2005, 29.

Unitary (or Identist) Pluralism

It is possible to climb life's mountain from any side, but when the top is reached, the trails converge. At the base, in the foothills of theology, ritual, and organizational structure, the religions are distinct. Differences in culture, history, geography, and collective temperament all make for diverse starting points. But beyond these differences, the same goal beckons. - Huston Smith[189]

The late John Hick (1922-2012) is arguably still the most well-known (and controversial) adherent of this position. As a result of interactions with other religious traditions, Hick moved away from his conservative Protestant upbringing into a pluralistic way of believing. He proposed a major shift in theology, one that would be as radical as the Copernican revolution, which shifted our belief in how the solar system works. As Copernicus showed us that Earth is not the unmoving center of the universe, Hick called for Christians to "shift from the dogma that Christianity is at the center to the realization that it is God ("Divine Reality," "Eternal One," "the Real") who is at the center, and that all religions . . . including our own, serve and revolve around him."[190] In other words, this would be a move away from a Christ-centered position to a theocentric one.

Hick's own thinking evolved as he moved from the use of "God" to other terms, such as "the Eternal One," "the Infinite," "the Absolute," "the Transcendent," "the Divine," and "the Ultimate." He finally settled on "the Real" as the term that could encompass both the personal and non-personal concepts of the Divine in various religious traditions.

It is not difficult to understand why Hick's proposal would be controversial. Although he offers a unitary position in which all religions can stand, he still leaves us with the question of what do with Jesus. On this question, Hick is among an increasing number of

---

[189] Smith, Huston, *The World's Religions: our great wisdom traditions.* New York: HarperSanFrancisco, 1991, 73.
[190] Hick, John, *God Has Many Names.* Philadelphia : Westminster Press, c1982.

theologians who have challenged traditional doctrines and have called for a revision of our understanding of Jesus as the incarnation of God, the only way to salvation. Again, this is an extremely sensitive subject to broach in the local congregation. However the interfaith landscape in which we find ourselves is making it increasingly difficult for us to ignore the impact that other religions are having on this claim.

Pluriform (or Differential) Pluralism

If practitioners of the world's religions are all mountain climbers, then they are on very different mountains, climbing very different peaks, and using very different tools and techniques in their ascents. – Stephen Prothero[191]

While both Stephen Prothero (*God Is Not One*)[192] and Stephen Kaplan (*Different Paths, Different Summits*)[193] address this position, Prothero's book is more of an attempt to convince us that there are distinctive differences among the world's religions and the answers they give to the different questions they ask. Kaplan actually provides a model for developing a pluralism that takes these differences into account: "a plurality of ultimate realities and a concomitant plurality of soteriological (salvation) experiences."[194] He identifies three categories within this plurality, their "summits" and their ways of reaching salvation/liberation: Being/Self (such as the Advaita Vedanta tradition of Hinduism); Becoming/Emptiness (Buddhism); and Theism/Rooted in an I-Thou relationship (the Abrahamic religions).

Process theologian John Cobb would also be included in this category. Cobb calls his position, which is based on the philosophy of Alfred North Whitehead (1861-1947), "complementary pluralism." He disagrees with those who argue that even though there are two different perceptions of ultimate reality – personal and non-personal –

---

[191] Prothero, Stephen, *God Is Not One: the eight rival religions that run the world-- and why their differences matter.* NY: HarperCollins, 2011, 11-12.
[192] Ibid.
[193] Kaplan, Stephen, *Different Paths, Different Summits.* Lanham, MD: Rowman & Littlefield Publishers, Inc., 2002
[194] Ibid, 117.

they indicate the same transcendent reality. In fact, he posits that there are at least two different ultimates.[195] One of these is the *formless* ultimate reality he calls "creativity" (a la Whitehead). It "has been called by names such as 'Emptiness' ('Sunyata') or 'Dharmakaya' by Buddhists, 'Nirguna Brahman' by Advaita Vedantists, 'the Godhead' by Meister Ekhart, and 'Being Itself' by Heidegger and Tillich (among others)."[196]

The other corresponds to what Whitehead calls "God." This ultimate "is not being itself but the supreme being. It is in-formed and the source of forms (such as truth, beauty and justice). It has been called "Amida Buddha," "Sambhogakaya," "Saguna Brahman," "Ishvara," "Yahweh," "Christ" and "Allah."[197]

Following then from the distinction between these two kinds of pluralism are two kinds of interfaith dialogues. There is a different kind of conversation among traditions with the same ultimate (such as Christians, Jews, Muslims and theistic Hindus) than there is when those with another ultimate are involved. Cobb explains:

> Consider the Buddhist claim that Gautama is the Buddha. That is a very different statement from the assertion that God was incarnate in Jesus. The Buddha is the one who is enlightened. To be enlightened is to realize the fundamental nature of reality, its insubstantiality, its relativity, its emptiness. . . . That Jesus was the incarnation of God does not deny that Gautama was the Enlightened One. In that vast complexity that is all that is, it may well be that God works creatively in all things and that at the same time, in the Buddhist sense, all things are empty. . . .

---

[195] Cobb developed the idea of two ultimates as a way to address theistic Christianity and non-theistic Buddhism. But he would also include a third ultimate: the cosmos or universe.

[196] Griffin, David Ray, ed., *Deep Religious Pluralism*. Louisville, KY: Westminster John Knox Press, 2005. 47.

[197] Ibid.

To affirm both that Jesus is the Christ and that Gautama is the Buddha is to move our understanding closer to the truth.[198]

Ethical Pluralism
Can we dare to live a reign of God that reaches not toward an imperialism of one religion – our own! – sweeping the planet, but that reaches toward a new form of community: a community made up of diverse religious communities, existing together in friendship? - Marjorie Suchocki[199]

Marjorie Suchocki is representative of this position. She believes that, even as we affirm pluralism, we must find a way of determining how religion provides for the wellbeing of the human community. She would have us make a shift away from discussions centered on ideology to those centered on ethics, in which justice would be "the fundamental criterion of value and the focus of dialogue and action among the religions."[200]

Writing from a feminist perspective in "In Search of Justice,"[201] she rejects any system that makes only one way of being normative for all. This applies to gender, race, class, sexual identity – and religion. The criticism of ethical pluralism, however, is this lack of normativity. Who sets the criteria for what is just? For example, there are differences within the religions concerning homosexuality, the role of women and contraception.

---

[198] Cobb, John, *Transforming Christianity and the World: A Way Beyond Absolutism and Relativism.* Maryknoll, NY: Orbis, 1999, 140.
[199] Suchocki, Marjorie. *Divinity & Diversity: A Christian Affirmation of Religious Pluralism.* Nashville: Abingdon Press, 2003, 86.
[200] Ibid.
[201] Ibid, 149.

The attempt of Gavin D'Costa at a simple definition notwithstanding, it is not easy to fit all the pluralist positions into his three categories. If you haven't torn your hair out by now, bear with me as I try to explain another way in which theologians have attempted to come to the table of interreligious dialogue from an explicitly Christian point of view.

In *The Many Faces of Christology*,[202] Tyron Inbody concludes that the choices of exclusivism, inclusivism, and pluralism are inadequate. He argues instead for what he calls confessional pluralism, defined by Anselm Min, Professor of Religion at Claremont Graduate University, as one "that encourages each religion to confess its distinctive beliefs and claims including the claim to finality. . . .," that does not "relativize the absolute claims of religions or demand . . . renunciation of such claims as a condition of interreligious dialogue."[203]

In this model there are two basic points:

1) Christianity (as are all religions) is contextual. We can see other traditions only through the lens of our own; we cannot claim to have a neutral perspective. Here in the West, we must even acknowledge that our lens is, in fact, Western. In this way, we do not presume to possess the entire truth. In other words, we can be pluralists, not from a universal perspective, but from an explicitly Christian one. We can affirm that no one religion has the complete truth, but that all of them embody part of the truth. This entails "a lack of finality and absoluteness" and an affirmation of "modesty about theological claims."[204] In other words, we can speak about other religions only from the perspective of our own particular views.

2) A confessional pluralist, who is a Christian, can affirm the universal significance of Christ and can enter interreligious dialogue from an explicitly Christian point of view. For instance, Inbody uses the Trinity to argue

---

[202] Inbody, Tyrone, *The Many Faces of Christology*, Nashville: Abingdon Press, 2002.

[203] Min, Anselm, "Dialectical Pluralism and Solidarity of Others: Towards as New Paradigm," *Journal of the American Academy of Religions*, Fall97, Vol. 65 Issue 3, 588.

[204] Inbody, Tyrone, *The Many Faces of Christology*, Nashville: Abingdon Press, 2002, 209.

that the triune nature of God would suggest that plurality is an irreducible fact about the world. The world is characterized by pluralism because unity-in-difference is the character of the Divine life itself.

Confessional pluralism can affirm that no one tradition possesses the complete truth; all religions embody part of that truth. It can also claim the universal significance of the revelation of God in Jesus. That may seem like an unreconcilable paradox, but John V. Taylor (1914-2001), the Anglican bishop and theologian, might help us out here. In his book *The Christlike God*, Taylor wrote:

> The different 'faces' of God which are set forth [in the various world religions] will seem in some respects to be mutually contradictory, and for a long time we may not be ready to guess how, if at all, they will be reconciled. I believe we can confidently leave that in the hands of the future if we will only persevere in the agenda for today. And for us who are Christians this is, quite simply, in reverent appreciation of the beliefs and prayers of others, to affirm that, whatever else he is, God is Christlike—humble and vulnerable in his love—and that we have found in that revelation the salvation that all peoples look for.[205]

By living with this paradox, we do not have to surrender our loyalty to the revelation we have received nor presume to be in possession of the entire truth.

These are very limited explanations of the basic pluralist positions. I encourage anyone with an interest in exploring them further to read the sources cited in the footnotes.

---

[205] Taylor, John V., *The Christlike God*. London: SCM Press; 2nd edition (November 9, 2011), 5, quoted in Lee M., "From Religious Diversity to Confessional Pluralism," thinkingreed.wordpress.com, December 18, 2011, https://thinkingreed.wordpress.com/2011/12/18/from-religious-diversity-to-confessional-pluralism (accessed March 4, 2016).

FOR REFLECTION:

- What did you find to be most strange or different or difficult to understand in this chapter?
- Is there a concept in this chapter that appeals to you, that you might like to explore further?
- Are there points on which you can agree with John Hick? On which you disagree? How would it be for you to be in a discussion group in which some participants held views such as Hicks' and some disagreed with him completely?
- With John Cobb? With Marjorie Suchocki?
- What would your touchstone be in an interfaith dialogue?

SUGGESTED READING:

- *Christians and Religious Pluralism: Patterns in the Christian Theology of Religions* by Alan Race   Chapter 4   "Pluralism"[206]

---

[206] Race.

Chapter 14   Radical Pluralism

The God present in Jesus is God himself. It is not that Jesus in his own being is identical with the God who is present in him.- Reginald H. Fuller[207]

I want to return now to process theologian John Cobb, who has written extensively on the subject of pluralism and the avoidance of relativism. Along with Complementary Pluralism (from the previous chapter), he has also written about Creative Transformation or Radical Pluralism. In this view, Christ is the Logos, the primordial nature of the Divine and the principle of creative transformation within all the religions.

Here we must step back a bit and look at Jesus and Christ in differing ways. In the same way that Pierre Teilhard de Chardin (1881-1955) wrote about the Cosmic Christ in 1916, Cobb wants us to expand our concept of Christ outward into the cosmos. In no way does he diminish the importance of the historical Jesus. What Cobb envisions is our faithfulness to the historical Jesus and the Logos that he incarnated.

In a column on the Process and Faith web site, Cobb responds to the question: "Which is more important, the historical Jesus or the Cosmic Christ?" His answer:

> In order to answer relatively simply, I will understand the Cosmic Christ to be what, in the prologue to John's gospel, is called the Logos. That identification answers the question. The Logos is more important. It is one with God, and there is no creation apart from the Logos.

> If we take Jesus seriously, we *must* assert the primacy of the Logos. Jesus points to God and calls on us to love God with all our being. Jesus is aware of the importance of his mission, but not in a way that is independent of the primary importance of God. In

[207] Reginald H. Fuller and Pheme Perkins, *Who is This Christ?* : Gospel Christology and Contemporary Faith. Philadelphia : Fortress Press, c1983, 8, quoted in S. J. Samartha, *One Christ – Many Religions: Toward a Revised.* Maryknoll, NY: Orbis Books, 1991.

other words, the importance of the historical Jesus is not in competition with the importance of the Logos . . . When we identify the Logos with the Cosmic Christ we are recognizing how intimately the importance of these two very different kinds of realities is bound together. This unity is at the heart of the Christian faith.[208]

Critics of this view contend that it is too abstract and that Cobb has removed a principle (Christ) from the human being (Jesus). They argue that for most Christians, Christ is not a principle, but a person - Jesus. However, in light of recent biblical scholarship, that argument may not be as valid as perhaps it once was. The work of the Jesus Seminar on the search for the historical Jesus, and subsequent work by Marcus Borg (*Meeting Jesus Again for the First Time*[209] and *The Heart of Christianity*)[210] and others have made biblical scholarship accessible to the general reader. The distinction is made between the Pre-Easter Jesus (Jesus of Nazareth) and the Post-Easter Jesus (Jesus the Christ) or the Jesus of history and the Christ of faith.

In a different vein, explorations into a more mystical understanding of Christ (Matthew Fox's *The Coming of the Cosmic Christ*)[211] and William Countryman's *The Mystical Way in the Fourth Gospel*)[212] may also serve to make Cobb's radical pluralism less abstract.

What Cobb accomplishes is a way to bring a cosmic Christian perspective to interreligious dialogue. Since the Logos (the Cosmos? the Tao?) is present in all religions, always creating, always opening us

---

[208] Cobb, John. "Historical Jesus or Cosmic Christ." processandfaith.org. http://oldsite.processandfaith.org/writings/ask-dr-cobb/2013-07/historical-jesus-or-cosmic-christ (accessed February 24, 2016).

[209] Borg, Marcus, *Meeting Jesus Again for the First Time*. San Francisco: HarperSanFrancisco, 1994.

[210] Borg, Marcus, *The Heart of Christianity: Rediscovering a Life of Faith*. New York: HarperCollins, 2003.

[211] Fox,.

[212] Countryman, L. William, *The Mystical Way in the Fourth Gospel: Crossing Over into God*. Valley Forge, PA: Trinity Press International, 1994.

up to change, then the possibilities of learning from one another and being transformed in the process are endless.

While there are indeed those who focus solely on the historical Jesus[213] and those who hold to a mysticism that would be more attuned to the Cosmic Christ, I believe that we can bring the two together in a way that enhances not only our own Christian path, but also our relationships with those of other paths. One creative expression of such a Christianity is the poem "Christpower"[214] by John Shelby Spong and Lucy Newton Boswell Negus. When I hear criticism of Spong and other progressive Christian writers as having no beliefs or not even being Christian, I refer them to this beautiful work. At the end of this chapter is just a brief excerpt (with thanks to Bishop Spong for his permission to include it), but I encourage you to read the entire work.

In conclusion, we may have to accept that there will always be a balancing act between particularity and relativity in our belief system. This may cause consternation for those who want definitive answers and absolute dogma. However, if we trust that the creative power of God – whether we call that Christ or Logos or Spirit – is at work in us, then we can be courageous in opening ourselves to the work of living into a pluralistic theology.

---

[213] There have been three so-called "quests for the historical Jesus since the 18th century. The latest, conducted by the Westar Institute has become famous for the Jesus Seminar and the subsequent book, The Five Gospels, which color code the words of Jesus by the probability of his actually having spoken them.

[214] Spong, John Shelby and Lucy Newton Boswell Negus. *Christpower*, Haworth, NJ, Saint Johann Press, 2007.

FOR REFLECTION:

- How do you think about the historic Jesus? About the Christ? Is there a difference?
- How might distinguishing between the two facilitate interreligious dialogue?
- What is your response to the poem *Christpower?*

SUGGESTED READING

- "The Pre- and Post-Easter Jesus"[215]
- "The Pre-Easter Jesus"[216]
- "The Post-Easter Jesus" [217]

---

[215] Howard, Cam. "A Portrait of Jesus." aportraitofjesus.org. http://www.aportraitofjesus.org/compare.shtml (accessed February 26, 2016).
[216] Howard, Cam. "A Portrait of Jesus." aportraitofjesus.org. http://www.aportraitofjesus.org/preeaster.shtml (accessed February 26, 2016).
[217]Howard, Cam. "A Portrait of Jesus." aportraitofjesus.org. http://www.aportraitofjesus.org/posteaster.shtml (accessed February 26, 2016).

"Christpower" (3 excerpts)

Far back beyond the beginning,
stretching out into the unknowable,
incomprehensible,
unfathomable depths, dark and void
of infinite eternity behind all history,
the Christpower was alive.

This was the
living,
bursting, pulsing,
generating, creating
smoldering, exploding
fusing, multiplying,
emerging, erupting,
pollenizing, inseminating,
heating, cooling
power of life itself: Christpower.
And it was good!

Finally, in the fullness of time,
within that human family,
one
unique and special human life appeared:
whole
complete
free
loving
living
being
at one
at peace
at rest.

In that life was seen with new intensity
that primal power of the universe,
Christpower.
And it was good!

Of that life people said: Jesus,
you are *the* Christ,
for in you we see
and feel
and experience
the living force of life
and love
and being
of God.

And even when the darkness of death overwhelmed him,
the power of life resurrected him;
for Christpower is life
eternal,
without beginning,
without ending.
It is the secret of creation.
It is the goal of humanity.

Here in this life we glimpse
that immortal
invisible
most blessed
most glorious
almighty life-giving force
of this universe
in startling completeness
in a single person.

PART V   The Mystic Heart

The paths are many, but the goal is the same. —Wayne Teasdale[218]

The categories and subcategories of exclusivism, inclusivism and pluralism are by no means the only ones available for our consideration. There is another way to approach the world's religions - from a metaphysical or mystical standpoint. While not an exclusively Christian approach, it does allow us to pursue this way of believing within our own Christian tradition. As Roman Catholic theologian Karl Rahner (1904-1984) said, "The Christian of the future will either be a mystic, one who has experienced something, or she will cease to be anything at all."[219]

In the next chapters, we will delve into Interspiritual Wisdom, which Brother Wayne Teasdale once said would be the religion of the third millennium. Following from that, we will look at what some are calling the coming Interspiritual Age. And finally, we will venture into the realm of Evolutionary Christianity.

---

[218] Teasdale, Wayne. *The Mystic Heart: Discovering a Universal Spirituality in the World's Religions.* Novato, CA: New World Library, 1999, 79.

[219] Rahner, Karl, "Christian Living Formerly and Today," in Theological Investigations VII, trans. David Bourke (New York: Herder and Herder, 1971), 15 as quoted in Painting the Stars: Science, religion and Evolving Faith, Session 7: "An Evolving Spirituality: Mysticism," 1.

Chapter 15   Interspiritual Wisdom

Wisdom is an ancient tradition, not limited to one particular religious expression but at the headwaters of all the great sacred paths...." – *Cynthia Bourgeault* [220]

With the publication of *The Mystic Heart*, in 1999, Brother Wayne Teasdale (1945 -2004) began a movement he called "interspirituality," a religious perspective that draws on the mystical core of the world's religions (he has also called it Global Spirituality and Interspiritual Wisdom). For Teasdale the real religion of humankind is spirituality. In light of the fact that many people today identify themselves as "spiritual, but not religious," he may have been on to something. He further maintains that since mystical spirituality is the origin of all the world's religions, interspirituality is the religion of the third millennium.

The key to the interspiritual movement is the prefix "inter." The essential spiritual interdependence of the religions exists because of the essential oneness of being and reality. All religions are part of the one cosmos in which everything is interrelated. "Inter" implies an openness and eagerness to communicate with people of other faiths, to learn from the wisdom of their traditions, and to assimilate that which is useful for one's own journey. Teasdale wrote that "Interspirituality is not a one-way street, but an intermystical intersection where insights cross back and forth, intermingle, and find new habitats."[221]

"Inter" is about responsibility to all of humankind and to all of creation itself, referring to the Dalai Lama's call to "universal responsibility to the global community of the earth, a responsibility that is both individual and collective.[222]

The heart of interspirituality is the recognition that there are many approaches to the spiritual journey. Proponents do not

---

[220] Bourgeault, Cynthia, *The Wisdom Way of Knowing: Reclaiming an Ancient Tradition to Awaken the Heart*. San Francisco: Jossey-Bass, 2003, 4.

[221] Teasdale, Wayne. *The Mystic Heart: Discovering a Universal Spirituality in the World's Religions*. Novato, CA: New World Library, 1999, 27.

[222] Tenzin Gyatso, the XIVth Dalai Lama, *The Global Community and the Need for Universal Responsibility*. Boston: Wisdom Publications, 1990, quoted in The Mystic Heart: Discovering a Universal Spirituality in the World's Religions. Novato, CA: New World Library, 1999, 27.

advocate for a rejection of the individual traditions or for the creation of a new superspirituality. A favorite saying is the Hindu aphorism: "The paths are many but the goal is the same." Hence, a faithful Christian is free to explore. There are no right or wrong answers, no how-to manuals. The tension to be managed is between the inner and outer journey, between contemplation and action. Teasdale describes it thus:

> By "interspiritual" is not meant the mixing of the various traditions but the possibility and actuality that we can learn and be nourished from more than our own mystical tradition. The note of interspiritual wisdom suggests that there is an underpinning, universal metaphysics. Traditionally, this is known as the *philosophia perennis*, – or perennial philosophy, the primordial tradition, the universal metaphysical tradition from which all particular religions are derived. It has often been referred to as "the transcendental unity of religions." Interspiritual wisdom is the practical part of the perennial philosophy, the inner, experiential core of it. It is the universal heritage of each one of us, and it becomes accessible to everyone based on our individual generosity to explore and our capacity to grow and be refined through the spiritual insights and practices of these various forms of spirituality: hence, the term "interspiritual wisdom.[223]

In 2001, at a weekend workshop at the Omega Institute in Rhinebeck, NY, I was privileged to sit at the feet of Huston Smith, the preeminent authority on world religions. Smith has not only studied and taught, but actually practiced Hindu Vedanta, Zen Buddhism, and Sufi Islam for more than ten years each—all the while remaining a member of the Methodist Church. At the workshop, after

---

[223] Teasdale, Wayne. "The Interspiritual Age: Practical Mysticism for the Third Millennium." interreligiousinsight.org. http://www.interreligiousinsight.org/April2006/TeasdaleEssay.html. (accessed February 24, 2016).

we had heard the fantastic stories of Smith's immersion in the world's religions, someone asked the question that was on my mind: "Why are you still a Christian?" His answer, which I cannot find in any of the "Famous Quotes" sites, has stayed with me over the years. He said, "Christianity is the string on which I hang my beads."

I later learned that Smith is an adherent of perennial philosophy, which holds that while the outward features of the world's religions are diverse and often contradictory, the inward features point to a single absolute, a transcendent unity. Those who are drawn to this perspective believe that perennial philosophy is very old, experienced in the very earliest faith expressions of humankind, as well as in the great religions of the world. If in God the religions converge above, below they are different. In other words, while the religions are the same in the spiritual sense, practical unity among the religions is not possible or even to be desired. Frithjof Schuon (1907–1998) writes:

> If the expression 'transcendent unity' is used, it means that the unity of the religious forms must be realized in a purely inward and spiritual way and without prejudice to any particular form. The antagonisms between these forms no more affect the one universal Truth than the antagonisms between opposing colors affect the transmission of the one uncolored light. Just as every color, by its negation of darkness and its affirmation of light, provides the possibility of discovering the ray that makes it visible and of tracing this ray back to its luminous source, so all forms, all symbols, all religions, all dogmas, by their negation of error and their affirmation of Truth, make it possible to follow the ray of Revelation, which is none other than the ray of the Intellect, back to its Divine Source.[224]

Although references to perennial philosophy go back to the 15th century, it was popularized in the late 20th century by writer and philosopher Aldous Huxley. His book *The Perennial Philosophy*,[225]

---

[224] Schuon, Fritjof. *The Transcendent Unity of Religions.* New York: Harper & Row, 1975, xxxi – xxxii.
[225] Huxley, Aldous. *The Perennial Philosophy.* London: Chatto & Windus, 1957.

published in 1957 became the central philosophy of the New Age Movement. But before we can dismiss it as too "woo woo" for mainline Christians, we have to give due consideration to the latest movement taking hold in our culture and in our congregations: interspirituality. Take, for example, this quote from a recent book by Rabbi Rami Shapiro entitled *Perennial Wisdom for the Spiritually Independent:* "There is only one reality (call it, among other names, God, Mother, Tao, Allah, Dharmakaya, Brahman, or Great Spirit) that is the source and substance of all creation."[226]

Consider also that when my congregation sponsored an event called "InterSpiritual Wisdom: Sharing the Mystic Heart" several years ago, we had to close registration because of space limitations. It was a two-day event, on Saturday and Sunday. The Saturday schedule included presenters from Buddhism, Christianity, Hinduism, Islam/Sufism and Judaism, who talked about their own spiritual beliefs and practices. But the best part was that they each taught a practice to the rest of us. Each segment was followed by a period of silence when we could practice on our own. On Sunday afternoon, there was a panel discussion and Q&A time, followed by an interspiritual zikr[227] led by our two Sufi presenters. The evaluations we received from attendees overwhelmingly indicated that they wanted more of the same.

Perhaps interspirituality is tapping into a need that our churches have been unwittingly neglecting. An important component of perennial philosophy is the distinction between the esoteric and the exoteric. For Frithjof Schuon (1907–1998), the dividing line between religions is not vertical, separating Christians from Buddhists, for example. Instead, the line that cuts across religions is horizontal, dividing them between esoterism above and exoterism below.

Esoterics derive meaning from the abstract. Exoterics derive meaning from forms that are more concrete. For example, esoterics may be drawn more to John's gospel for Christmas Day, which

---

[226] Shapiro, Rami, *Perennial Wisdom for the Spiritually Independent.* (Woodstock, VT: SkyLight Paths, 2013), Kindle edition, location 84.

[227] Zikr (Arabic for 'remembrance') is a form of devotion, in which participants are absorbed in the rhythmic repetition of the Divine name or attributes of the Divine.

instead of a birth story soars in cosmic grandeur: "In the beginning was the Word." Exoterics delight in the details of Luke's Christmas Eve story, with details of shepherds and swaddling cloths.

The esoteric/exoteric distinction is similar to the difference between apophatic and kataphatic spirituality. Apophatic spirituality is often called "negative spirituality," because it approaches the Divine as Mystery - beyond words, images, symbols, rituals, etc. Kataphatic spirituality approaches the Divine through just these means and affirms positive knowledge about God - what we can say about who God is. Apophatic theology, being more intuitive, affirms God as rationally unknowable. Kataphatic theology presumes a certain amount of rational knowledge derived from how God manifests God's Self in the world.

While probably most of us are familiar with an exoteric/kataphatic form of Christianity (our scriptures, books, liturgies, hymns, etc.), both forms can be found in the Christian tradition. Many people are finding that the recovery of apopahtic writings and practices (or a combination of both) to be more attuned with their spiritual needs.

This is a perspective that may appeal to those more attracted to mysticism than to a dogmatic faith. It also removes the difficulties of an interfaith theology and reframes the conversation in terms of an interfaith spirituality. However it does not address, nor does it claim to address, the issues of differences within the traditions.

FOR REFLECTION:

- Would you describe yourself as being more of an esoteric or an exoteric?
- What are some of the ways you find meaning in either an esoteric or exoteric way?
- What do you think are the benefits of Interspirituality? The detriments or dangers?

SUGGESTED READING

- *The Mystic Heart* by Wayne Teasdale[228]

---

[228] Teasdale, Wayne, *The Mystic Heart: Discovering a Universal Spirituality in the World's Religions.* Novato, CA: New World Library, 1999.

Chapter 16   The Coming Interspiritual Age

The world's interspiritual pioneers envision the emergence of a new axial age, reconciling destructive tensions that have plagued the human family and awakening a transformed new era of enlightened understanding. - Interspirit Alliance[229]

Although Teasdale died in 2004, others have picked up the mantle. Kurt Johnson and David Robert Ord's 2013 book, *The Coming Interspiritual Age*,[230] has been described as the follow-up to *The Mystic Heart. The Interspirit Alliance*, founded by Bruce Schuman, invites us to join the movement into a "new era of enlightened understanding." They not only agree with Brother Teasdale's characterization of interspirituality as the religion of the third millennium, they predict that humankind is about to enter into a new age of interdependence among the people of the world.

Again, before we dismiss this movement as too "New Age-y" or simply a remnant of the1960's Age of Aquarius, we need to know that this prediction is actually based on social theory. Teasdale and others who consider themselves interspiritual pioneers would have us look back to a major paradigm shift in human consciousness called the Axial Age and consider that we are now in the first stages of a second such shift.

Shift Happens

First, a word about paradigm shifts. This is a term that became popular in the church a few decades ago. As a pastor, I became very familiar with the challenge to make the transition from a church that had been designed for Baby Boomers to one that would meet the needs of Generation X. Little did I know that in our drive to be relevant, we would be required to shift again and again, as each subsequent generation presented its unique characteristics and needs.

However, theologians and philosophers would have us understand that all of these small shifts are now taking place within a

---

[229] "Integral Activism: The Coming Interspiritual Age." interspirit.net. http://www.interspirit.net/alliance/index.cfm (accessed February 26, 2016).

[230] Johnson, Kurt and David Robert Ord, *The Coming Interspiritual Age*. Vancouver: Namaste Publishing, 2013.

much larger one that affects all of our institutions on a global scale. Roman Catholic theologian Hans Küng calls it a Macro-Paradigm-Shift, which began towards the end of the 20th century. In this new era, humanity is coming to understand the world and human responsibility in global, not local terms. This shift is the impetus for working together for the betterment of the world. His insight, "Peace among the religions is the prerequisite to peace among the nations," backs up his call for an ecumenical theology:

> a theology that no longer sees in every other theology the opponent, but the partner, and that is intent not on separation but on understanding, and this in two directions: inwards, for the domain of world ecumene between the churches, among Christians; and outwards, for the domain of world ecumene outside the Church, outside of Christianity, with its different religions, ideologies and disciplines.[231]

Ewart Cousins (1927-2009), another Catholic theologian goes so far as to call it the beginning of nothing less than a Second Axial Age and calls us to get with the program: ". . . I believe the religions of the world--must face together the challenges of the Second Axial Period."[232]

But what are these people talking about? The word axial comes from German philosopher Karl Jaspers' use of the German word 'achse,' which means pivotal. The theory is that during certain periods of history there have been major changes in the political, philosophical and religious systems of the world. Cousins, Teasdale, Schuman and many others claim that we are now in such a time. But in order to understand this reference to a new age, we have to understand the former one, as well as the time preceding it.

---

[231] Kung, Hans, *Theology for the Third Millennium.* New York: Doubleday, 1988, 204.

[232] Cousins, Ewert, "Religions of the World: Teilhard and the second axial turning." interreligiousinsight.org.
http://www.interreligiousinsight.org/October2006/Cousins10-06.pdf (accessed February 28, 2016).

Before the arrival of the first axial age, human culture was primarily tribal. Being part of the tribe meant not only knowing one's identity, but also having protection from other tribes. The lives of pre-axial people were intimately connected to the life cycles of nature and to the cosmos. Harmony in the relationship between human beings and the natural world was expressed in myth and ritual. However, this harmony extended only to members of one's own tribe. Other tribes were considered "other" and usually with hostility.

The period in history from about 800 BCE to 100 CE (the date range varies among historians) is characterized by the emergence of new philosophical and religious thought throughout the region from the eastern Mediterranean to China. Tribal cultures were faced with the rise of urban life. They had to develop ethical systems that could transcend the rules of the various tribes. Consider the phenomenon of the Golden Rule (or the Ethic of Reciprocity), which is expressed throughout religions, philosophy and ethical systems. This idea that we should treat others as we would like to be treated ourselves emerged during the Axial Age. For example:

- From the Prophet Muhammad: "Not one of you truly believes until you wish for others what you wish for yourself."[233]
- From the Buddha: "Treat not others in ways that you yourself would find hurtful."[234]
- From Confucius: "What I do not wish others to do to me, that also I wish not to do to them"[235]
- From Zoroaster: "That which is good for all and any one, for whomsoever—that is good for me...what I hold good for self, I should for all. Only Law Universal is true Law."[236]

Of course, in the Jewish scriptures, the book of Leviticus says, "You shall love your neighbor as yourself."[237] And in the New Testament Jesus says, "In everything, do to others as you would have them do to

---

[233] Hadith
[234] Udana-Varga 5.18
[235] Analects, 5.11
[236] Gathas, 43.1
[237] Lev. 19: 18

you; for this is the law and the prophets."[238] With all this evidence, it should be easy for us to see this teaching as interspiritual wisdom!

The first Axial age ushered in a radically new form of consciousness. The great religions of the world are the product of the Axial Period. Hinduism, Buddhism, Taoism, Confucianism, and Judaism all took shape in their classical forms during this period; and Judaism provided the base for the later emergence of Christianity and Islam.

The New Axial Age

According to thinkers like Wayne Teasdale, Karen Armstrong and Leonard J. Swidler, we are now entering a pivotal time as momentous as the First Axial Age. Wayne Teasdale wrote:

> We are at the threshold of a new age, a Second Axial Age, a decisive period that will be characterized by a deep sense of community among the religions – of interspiritual wisdom – and a profound commitment to environmental justice. . . . the Second Axial Age names these two fundamental shifts in consciousness that imply one another: the emergence of interspiritual wisdom from the discovery of community among members of the various religions, and the serious focus on the ultimate value of and concern for the Earth.[239]

Karen Armstrong, whose 2006 book *The Great Transformation: The Beginning of Our Religious Traditions* chronicled the development of religion in the First Axial Age, has written:

---

[238] Matthew 7:12.

[239] Teasdale, Wayne. "The Interspiritual Age: Practical Mysticism for the Third Millennium." interreligiousinsight.org. http://www.interreligiousinsight.org/April2006/TeasdaleEssay.html (accessed February 26, 2016).

All over the world, people are struggling with these new conditions and have been forced to reassess their religious traditions, which were designed for a very different type of society. They are finding that the old forms of faith no longer work for them; they cannot provide the enlightenment and consolation that human beings seem to need. As a result, men and women are trying to find new ways of being religious. Like the reformers and prophets of the first Axial Age, they are attempting to build upon the insights of the past in a way that will take human beings forward into the new world they have created for themselves.[240]

And Leonard Swidler, Professor of Catholic Thought and Interreligious Dialogue at Temple University, Philadelphia, PA, wrote:

Following the lead of Ewert Cousins . . . we can discern another transformation of consciousness, which is so profound and far-reaching that he calls it the Second Axial Period. Like the first it is happening simultaneously around the earth, and like the first it will shape the horizon of consciousness for future centuries. Not surprisingly, too, it will have great significance for world religions, which were constituted in the First Axial Period. However, the new form of consciousness is different from that of the First Axial Period. Then it was individual consciousness, now it is global consciousness.[241]

[240] Roemischer, Jessica. "A New Axial Age: Karen Armstrong on the History—and the Future—of God." adishakti.org.
http://www.adishakti.org/_/a_new_axial_age_by_karen_armstrong.htm. (accessed February 24, 2016).
[241] "The Age of Global Dialogue." Swidler, Leonard. uni-marburg.de.
https://www.uni-marburg.de/fb03/ivk/mjr/pdfs/1996/articles/Swidler1996.pdf (accessed February 24, 2016).

To sum up, some of the main characteristics of the emerging paradigm are:

1. It is global. Humanity is seen as a single tribe and this one tribe is interconnected with the total cosmos.

2. It is an age of dialogue, not monologue. Instead of talking only with those like us, we meet with people of differing convictions, not as opponent, but in order to listen, share and learn from one another.

3. It will be characterized by a deep commitment to environmental justice, including a shift from an exclusively anthropocentric view to one which sees humanity in interdependent relationship with all other life forms and with the Earth itself.

4. It will involve a redefinition of religion. Many of the answers given in the past do not address questions being asked today. Just as Christianity moved from a Jewish way of thinking into one of Greek philospophy (which produced the 'substance' language of the Nicene Creed), we are now moving into a new way of reflecting on theological matters. Interspiritual pioneers, such as Teasdale, Johnson and Ord believe that interspirituality is the form that it will take.

FOR RELECTION:

- What is your reaction to those who believe we are entering a Macro-Paradigm Shift or a Second Axial Age?
- What is your impression of the four main characteristics of the emerging paradigm listed above?
- Can you think of any questions being asked by people today that are not being answered by traditional religion?
- Would you agree with Brother Wayne Teasdale that interspirituality is the religion of the third millennium? Why or why not?

SUGGESTED READING:

- *The Great Transformation: The Beginning of Our Religious Traditions* by Karen Armstrong[242]
- "A New Axial Age: Karen Armstrong on the History—and the Future—of God" by Jessica Roemischer[243]

---

[242] Armstrong, Karen, *The Great Transformation: The Beginning of Our Religious Traditions.* New York : Alfred A. Knopf, 2006.

[243] Roemischer, Jessica. "A New Axial Age: Karen Armstrong on the History—and the Future—of God." adishakti.org. http://www.adishakti.org/_/a_new_axial_age_by_karen_armstrong.htm (accessed February 26, 2016).

Chapter 17   Evolutionary Christianity

. . . God is in the evolutionary process and the evolutionary process is in God. – Bruce Sanguin[244]

In February 2006, at First United Lutheran Church we observed our first Evolution Sunday. I had received an invitation from Michael Zimmerman, then a biology professor at the University of Wisconsin–Oshkosh, to sign onto the Clergy Letter Project. This had originally begun as an effort to rescind an anti-evolution policy by a local school board. The letter, describing how religion and science are not incompatible, was initially sent only to Christian clergy for signatures. But after the success of the campaign, Zimmerman began gathering even more signators and organized the first Evolution Sunday. Its purpose: to encourage faith communities to engage in some way the role of science and religion on the weekend nearest to Charles Darwin's birthday on February 12. In 2008, it was renamed Evolution Weekend to include more religious traditions.

On that first Evolution Sunday, one member wondered why we were doing it since, he said, no one at First United needed to be convinced of the compatibility of science and religion; after all we have scientists in our congregation. However, I felt that it was important to take a public stand on the issue, which is still controversial in many places. We have been observing the day ever since, although I have to say it has been rather a perfunctory effort.

That is until I began to learn about evolutionary Christianity. Evolutionary spirituality goes past the realm of mere support of evolution theory and more deeply into the heart of Mystery. It does not necessarily have to be Christian, but for those thinkers who are Christian, the Christ of the cosmos is a central figure.

For many people, when they hear "evolution," they think only about the history of the earth and the development of human life. But evolutionary Christianity expands on the biological and geological data and includes findings of social scientists who recognize stages of development beyond the physical, such as the cultural, social and political. It also accepts as fact that, just as the universe itself is

---

[244] Sanguin, Bruce, *Darwin, Divinity and the Dance of the Cosmos*. Kelowna, BC: CopperHouse, 2007, 111.

evolving, so is Christianity and so is the Church. As Bruce Sanguin writes:

> We are meant to evolve. If the Spirit is involved in the evolutionary process – as I believe is the case – then we need to start thinking about our lives in Christ through an evolutionary lens.[245]

Evolutionary Christians, such as Sanguin, Ilia Delio, Michael Morwood and Ursula King are leading the way forward, following in the footsteps of the likes of the late Passionist priest Thomas Berry (1914-2009) and the paleontologist and Jesuit priest, Pierre Teilhard de Chardin (1881-1955). They see the evolution of the universe as an ongoing sacred story that connects all people, all cultures, all religions and virtually all of creation.

Evolutionary spirituality offers a middle way between a scientific position that is not willing to allow for the presence of any spiritual dimension and a religious one that insists that there is a divine blueprint that God put in place "in the beginning." Evolutionary Christianity also invites us to move from a redemption-centered theology to a creation-centered, evolutionary model.

In order to make that shift, we need to understand the Christ of the cosmos, what Pierre Teilhard de Chardin meant when he wrote, "Christ has a cosmic body that extends throughout the whole universe"[246] and Franciscan Sister Ilia Delio, who said, "Christ is the evolver, the centrating energy of the evolutionary movement."[247]

I admit that the shift can be a work in progress. For example, a number of years ago, our worship planning team was wrestling with what to call Christ the King Sunday. We had been trying to move away from both exclusively male language and from hierarchical concepts of divinity. A beloved colleague, the Rev. Paul Brenner (now

---

[245] Sanguin, Bruce, *The Emerging Church*, Kelowna, BC: Wood Lake Publishing Inc., 2014, 14.

[246] Teilhard de Chardin, Pierre, *Writings in Time of War*. New York: Harper & Row, 1968, 58.

[247] Delio, Ilia, "Painting the Stars" Session 4: An Evolving Faith," 2013. DVD. http://www.livingthequestions.com (accessed February 26, 2016).

deceased) had come up with the title "The Feast of the Culmination of All Things in Christ." I thought that theologically the name said it all, but when someone began referring to Jesus as "The Culminator," I realized it wouldn't fly.

Our next attempt to reimagine Christ the King was to use the title "The Cosmic Christ." But that was not well received by the congregation either. We finally settled on "Christ Anointed," although I am not convinced that "The Cosmic Christ" is not the more appropriate title.

For many people within the Church, however, the term "Cosmic Christ" is tinged with "New Age" undertones. Our response to such things is often, "That's just too woo-woo for me," and we dismiss them as flaky nonsense. And while it is true that one can find references to the Cosmic Christ by New Age thinkers, the name itself is not new at all.

Some think that it began with the 1988 publication of *The Coming of the Cosmic Christ*[248] by former Dominican now Episcopal priest Matthew Fox. Fox' main contribution to the current scene is a renewed interest in Creation-centered spirituality. But consider that a book entitled *The Cosmic Christ: From Paul to Teilhard* was published all the way back in 1968. The author, George A. Maloney (1924 – 2005) was a former Jesuit priest, and at the time of his death, a priest in the Eastern Orthodox Church. The long list of Father Maloney's books includes *Entering Into the Heart of Jesus*[249] and *Abiding in the Indwelling Trinity*,[250] which place him securely within the ranks of tradition, albeit one infused with Christian mysticism.

Chapters of the book include the biblical roots of the Cosmic Christ ("Paul's Dimensions of Salvation" and "The Cosmic Logos of John") and historical treatments of early Church fathers. But to my mind, it is the chapter entitled "The Cosmic Christology of Teilhard de Chardin" that links us securely to recent interest in the Cosmic Christ, particularly as religion relates to modern scientific discoveries.

Pierre Teilhard de Chardin was a scientist, trained in geology,

---

[248] Fox.

[249] Maloney, George A., *Entering Into the Heart of Jesus*, NY: Alba House, 1988.

[250] Maloney, George A., *Abiding in the Indwelling Trinity*, Mahwah, NJ: Paulist Press, 2005.

botany, zoology and paleontology. He participated in the discovery of Peking Man in 1926. He was also a Jesuit priest. In his 1929 book, *The Divine Milieu*, Teilhard (as he was known) synthesized scientific discoveries of his day with what he believed about God and how God was at work in the world. As is often the case with new ideas, his religious superiors would not allow the book to be published. The French edition was not published until after his death. The English translation was not available until 1960.

Today, readers of Matthew Fox, Marcus Borg, Sallie McFague and others would recognize Teilhard as a panentheist. His "Divine Milieu" is the body of God in which we live and move and have our being. This is not pantheism, in which there is no difference between everything around us and God. Rather, as Louis M. Savary describes so well in *Teilhard de Chardin – The Divine Milieu Explained: A Spirituality for the 21st Century*,

> A milieu is as penetrating and omnipresent as the air we breathe; yet we mostly take it for granted. We simply forget about the atmosphere, even though we are dependent upon it at every moment. As soon as we are deprived of oxygen to breathe, we quickly become aware of our need for it. Fish live in a milieu of water yet are unaware of its importance until they are taken out of it. For Teilhard, the most important spiritual fact of our existence is that at every minute you and I are swimming in a divine sea. Fortunately we can't be taken out of it. At every moment we are inhaling and exhaling the divine life. In the divine milieu we live and move and have our being. While it is true that God is always "in heaven" (transcendent) and also always "within us" (immanent), the more important fact is that we are always living and moving *within* the divine milieu.[251]

---

[251] Savary, Louis, *Teilhard de Chardin - The Divine Milieu Explained: A Spirituality for the 21st Century* Mahwah, NJ: Paulist Press, 2007, 18.

For Teilhard, the divine milieu is the Cosmic Christ. He resonates with the theology of St. Paul and others in passages such as: "So all of us, in union with Christ, form one body. And as members of that one body, we belong to each other"[252] and

> Christ is the image of the unseen God and the firstborn of all creation, for in Christ were created all things in heaven and on earth: everything visible and invisible, thrones, dominations, sovereignties, Powers—all things were created through Christ and for Christ. Before anything was created, Christ existed, and all things hold together in Christ.[253]

Sometimes using the names The Total Christ, The Universal Christ, the Christic, as well as the Cosmic Christ, Teilhard's understanding is of a presence of Christ in the universe that is evolving toward what he called the Omega Point, the culmination of creation, which is Christ's body (Ah ha! Pastor Brenner was thoroughly Teilhardian!).

But we can go still further back than Teilhard de Chardin. Hildegard of Bingen, along with other medieval mystics, expressed her experience of the Cosmic Christ. Through music, writing and painting, Hildegard formulated a cosmological theology that transcends male/female, human/divine, earth/heaven duality. Her visionary work, *Liber Divinorum Operum (Book of Divine Works),* is a result of what she called "an extraordinary mystical vision" in which she experienced insights into the cosmic dimensions of the Prologue to John's Gospel. One of the ten visions Hildegard illustrates in this work is of the cosmos, with a human figure at its center, inside the womb of divinity: a visual portrayal of the Cosmic Christ. Hildegard explains:

> From the primordial source of Divine Love, in whom
> the cosmic order rests, shines her exceedingly precise

---

[252] *The Inclusive Bible*, Romans 12:5
[253] *The Inclusive Bible*, Colossians 1:15-17

ordering of things. It comes to light in ever-new ways, holding and tending everything there is."[254]

Contemporary interest in the Cosmic Christ has become the theological foundation, for not only creation-centered and evolutionary theologies, but also a spiritual approach to the world's religions. Matthew Fox, for example, sees the Cosmic Christ as:

> the light in every being in the universe. In other words, every being in the universe is the image of God. The 'Buddha Nature' is a parallel name for this same idea within Buddhism, and this idea also exists at the heart of the Jewish tradition.[255]

Ilia Delio, who bases her theology of the "ecological Christ" on her understanding of the cosmic Christ mysticism of St. Francis and St. Bonaventure, concludes:

> Every age must discover Christ anew. Our traditional christology—the formal study of Jesus Christ—was formulated in the fourth and fifth centuries: Jesus Christ is true God and true man, fully divine and fully human without change, without confusion, without separation, without division, two natures in one person. The language is a mixture of the New Testament, Greek metaphysics, and Plato and Aristotle, which reflects an understanding of the universe as fixed and unchanging, not dynamic and evolving.[256]

---

[254] Craine, Renate, *Hildegard: Prophet of the Cosmic Christ*. New York: Crossroad Publishing Company, 1997, 148.

[255] Fox, Matthew. "Love Is Stronger than Stewardship: A Cosmic Christ Path to Planetary Survival." tikkun.org. http://www.tikkun.org/nextgen/love-is-stronger-than-stewardship-a-cosmic-christ-path-to-planetary-survival. (accessed February 24, 2016).

256 U.S. Catholic, "Universal Savior: Ilia Delio reimagines Christ." uscatholic.org. http://www.uscatholic.org/church/2011/03/universal-savior-ilia-delio-reimagines-christ. (accessed February 24, 2016).

Evolutionary Christianity might seem like a foreign language to many of us. But if we listen to these thinkers with an open heart and mind, we may indeed discover Christ anew – and find yet another way into our *inter*faith and *intra*faith explorations.

FOR REFLECTION:

- Can you think of other biblical passages that reflect a cosmic view of Christ?
- What are the implications for you of living in the "Divine Milieu"?
- How do you feel about a concept of Christ that is bigger than Christianity?

SUGGESTED READING:

- *Teilhard de Chardin -The Divine Milieu Explained: A Spirituality for the 21ˢᵗ Century* by Louis M. Savory[257]
- *If Darwin Prayed: Prayers for Evolutionary Mystics* by Bruce Sanguin[258]

SUGGESTED VIEWING:

- *Painting the Stars: Science, Religion and an Evolving Faith*[259]

---

[257] Savory, Louis M., *Teilhard de Chardin -The Divine Milieu Explained: A Spirituality for the 21ˢᵗ Century*. Mahwah, NJ: Paulist Press, 2007.
[258] Sanguin, Bruce, *If Darwin Prayed: Prayers for Evolutionary Mystics*. evans and sanguin publishing, 2010.
[259] "Painting the Stars" is a DVD-based curriculum available from http://www.livingthequestions.com.

PART VI Passing Over and Coming Back: One Pastor's Story

. . . the spiritual adventure of our time. - John Dunne[260]

Now we begin to delve into some practical applications of our theological work. This section will include stories from my own experience of working with congregations in both meeting members of other faith groups ("passing over") and reflecting on the experiences ("coming back"). I discovered this concept in John Dunne's *The Way of All the Earth*:

> What seems to be occurring is a phenomenon we might call 'passing over,' passing from one culture to another, from one way of life to another, from one religion to another. Passing over is a shifting of standpoint, a going over to the standpoint of another culture, another way of life, another religion. It is followed by an equal and opposite process we might call 'coming back,' coming back with new insight to one's own culture, one's own way of life, one's own religion. . . Passing over and coming back, it seems, is the spiritual adventure of our time.[261]

Dunne, like Frederick Buechner, believes that perspective is always autobiographical. As we pass over into experiences of other lives, we must eventually come back to our own. Graduate Theological Union professor Judith Berling[262] also uses this kind of language. She describes the two poles of the interreligious learning

---

[260] Dunne, John, *The Way of All the Earth*. New York: Macmillan, 1972, ix.

[261] Ibid.

[262] "The Graduate Theological Union is an ecumenical and interreligious crossroads, building bridges among Christian denominations and other faith traditions, and dedicated to educating students for teaching, research, ministry, and service. We seek to achieve our mission in two ways: as a graduate school offering academic programs in a wide range of fields in theology and religious studies, and as the largest partnership of seminaries and graduate schools in the United States. The GTU flourishes as a haven for interdisciplinary religious thought, study, and practice, making a tangible difference for the greatest good – and serving as the place where religion meets the world." http://gtu.edu/about

process as 1) understanding another religion faithfully, and 2) reappropriating Christian tradition in light of new understandings and relationships.[263] She cites the example of a course she teaches on Chinese spiritual traditions:

> I help students cross a bridge to explore Chinese territory, but stay with them also on the journey back, reflecting on what difference the journey has made.[264]

The role of the teacher/leader is, as Berling says, to address the issues and concerns of the students, so that the course always "connects back to them."[265] This makes the process a circular movement that has no definitive ending. Dunne also describes this movement:

> No matter how conscious a man is . . . he is never fully conscious; no matter how much a man knows, he never knows everything a man can know. So each voyage around his world his path is a different turn on the spiral and he makes new discoveries.[266]

The "coming back" process is the way into the *intra*faith conversation: what questions came up; where were the similarities and differences? The following chapters will describe a few of these stories. In no way do I intend to suggest that all congregations will be able to replicate these experiences. Each community must create its own opportunities that are appropriate for them.

---

[263] Berling, Judith, *Understanding Other Worlds: A Guide for Interreligious Education.* Maryknoll, NY: Orbis Books, 2004), 64.

[264] Berling, Judith, "Getting Out of the Way: A Strategy for Engaging Students in Collaborative Learning," *Teaching Theology & Religion*, Volume 1, Issue 1, page 32, February 1998.

[265] Ibid.

[266] Dunne, John, *The Way of All the Earth.* New York: Macmillan, 1972, 198.

Chapter 18 A Christian/Buddhist Encounter

The number one obstacle to interfaith is a bad relationship with one's own faith. —
Dalai Lama

Although I had been involved in interfaith activities before, my first foray into "passing over/coming back" was putting together a group intentionally comprised of members of two different traditions. This would be the group that would be the practicum for my doctoral thesis[267] at the Pacific School of Religion in Berkeley, CA. One of the traditions would be Christian; I recruited participants from the church I was attending at the time, University Lutheran Chapel in Berkeley. By surveying those who agreed to participate, I determined that the other tradition would be Buddhism.

It was more of a challenge to find the Buddhist participants. Because I was new to the area, I did not have the same network of interfaith connections that I had had back in Buffalo. I had to spend more time making personal contacts, explaining the project further and developing a trust level with people who did not know me. Once the word began to spread, however, I began to receive calls and e-mails expressing interest in the group. A major advance came when a member of the Buddhist Peace Fellowship (BPF) who had worked with me on an interfaith event planning committee agreed to be part of my group. She also invited me to attend a BPF meeting where I could explain my project and hopefully get the word out through their network. Once I became known (and with an insider's "endorsement") the information about the project went out over several e-mail networks and I received even more e-mails and phone calls from people asking for more information about the project. In light of these inquiries, I decided to hold an informational gathering in the fall for anyone who was interested. In the meantime, I scheduled individual interviews with those who had already made a commitment to be in the group, mainly to learn their religious backgrounds and the reasons for their interest.

---

[267] Susan M. Strouse, "Passing Over and Coming Back: What Does It Mean to Be a Christian in an Interfaith World?" (doctor of ministry thesis, Pacific School of Religion, 2005).

I ended up with sixteen people, excluding myself. Seven of the Christians came from the Chapel; the eighth (who happened to be my landlady) had no particular church affiliation but identified as a Christian and had done extensive reading about other traditions. The eight Buddhists came from several different communities and had differing understandings of Buddhism. All were western converts. One was a Zen Roshi[268] from a secular Jewish background, who offered to assist with group facilitation. Most were from the Theravadan vipassana tradition. One identified himself as both a Christian and a Buddhist, and one did not identify with any particular tradition.

Prior to our first meeting, I conducted individual interviews. In addition to asking questions about religious background in order to get to know them better, I asked each one to talk about their interest in being part of this group. Some of the responses from the Christian participants were:

- I have friends who are married to Buddhists.
- I am a seeker, have always been interested in people from other countries
- Christian exclusivity is offensive.
- People in the United States need to know more about other faiths.
- I am interested in Buddhism because I struggle with the idea of a personal God.
- I want to be more knowledgeable; I am bothered by proselytizing.
- Christianity is not the only thing happening. I'm interested in anything that works toward peace.
- I've always believed we will all go to heaven; we have to foster the dream.

---

[268] A trained Zen master or teacher; it literally means "venerable teacher."

Buddhist responses included:

- I want to know how Christians perceive Buddhism.
- I'm exploring being both Christian and Buddhist.
- Does Buddhist practice have any bearing on Christianity?
- I want to support this project and help others learn about Buddhism.
- It's important to be in this kind of dialogue.
- I was baptized and married in the Roman Catholic church and want to explore how that relates to my long-time Buddhist practice.

At our first session, it was important to set the stage for all of our work. My first intention was to create a safe environment in which participants would feel free to express opinions and beliefs without fear of being "wrong," to initiate a conversation in which I was not an authority who would give them answers, but a participant in the process. Hospitality was key. A cardinal rule of interfaith gathering is to always have food and music! In the beginning, especially, this helped break the ice and create a sense of community.

Introductions always take a long time, but it was an important part of the group-building process to listen to each person's background and reasons for being part of the group. We then read and agreed to the "Guidelines for Conversation." (Appendix B)

I introduced them to Dunne's concept "passing/over and coming back," although it quickly became clear that this would be (in the words of my faculty advisor, Fumitaka Matsuoka) "a messy process." The boundaries in the group were not as clearly defined as I had expected. All of the Buddhists were western converts from either Judaism or Christianity. One claimed adherence to both Christianity and Buddhism. Another professed to be Christian but had no background in a particular church. Some of the Buddhists seemed to have a greater interest in pursuing questions about God and Jesus - remnants of previous (and current) affiliations. Buddhist converts and Buddhist/Christians had personal questions about Christianity. I realized that the "passing over" would not be only the scheduled ritual experiences we might have, but would perhaps be, more importantly, the personal lives and experiences of each of the participants.

Our first collaborative task was to create a list of topics to use as a guide for the rest of the sessions. The group was very engaged and quickly listed their goals, expectations, and hopes. Some of these were:

- Learn about Buddhism (various traditions)
- Who is Christ? Who is God?
- Who is Christ to me (personally)?
- How is Buddhism manifested in daily life?
- Is Buddha God?
- Christian route to forgiveness / Buddhist route to forgiveness
- What is faith?
- What is prayer?
- Theism, non-duality, interdependence
- Christian superiority over nature

I definitely had no lack of subject matter for our time together!

Our subsequent sessions included conversation about some of the above topics. But I also used art as a way of getting us out of our "left brain" functioning. One activity was during our discussion of Ultimate Reality, the "god" question that was inherent in several topics on the list. I asked them to express their concept of Ultimate Reality in the form of a mandala. I gave a brief explanation of mandalas, showed them some examples, including Martin Luther's seal, the Luther Rose. Surprisingly, the Lutherans were not familiar with it. The Buddhists, however, were enchanted with the symbol, especially presented as a mandala.

Some were hesitant ("I'm not an artist!") but all of them got into it quickly. In fact they appeared to have quite a fun time with all of the various arts and crafts supplies I had brought. When they were finished, most were eager to share their concepts of Ultimate Reality, which were insightful and creative. Only two were expressions of any kind of doctrine - both from Buddhists. The Zen Roshi, who had been raised as a secular Jew, created a Tree of Life in the mandala exercise, much to his surprise. This was in no way what he had intended to create and he found himself reconnecting with his Jewish roots.

The first "passing over" experience for the Buddhists was attending the Sunday morning service at the Chapel. First up for the Christians was Zen meditation conducted by our resident Roshi. We spent the next session "coming back" and processing our experiences. One interesting note was the discontent of some of the Buddhists from the Vipassana tradition, who did not particularly appreciate the Zen experience. In fact some of them worried that the Christians were not getting the "right" version of Buddhism (this also happened later when our guest was Rev. Sasaki from the Buddhist Church of San Francisco, which is a Japanese Pure Land congregation). The learning for the Christians was that we're not the only ones who have differences among "denominations. Other "passing over" experiences included visits to the Berkeley Buddhist Monastery, once for a Chinese Buddhist service and twice for Vipassana meditation.

Another "right brain" activity was designed to get at the "Who is Christ?" question. I had collected pictures depicting various aspects of Jesus (Nativity, teaching, healing, crucifixion, the Risen Christ, the Ascension, etc.) in various works of art. I spread these out on a table and invited them to peruse the pictures. As they looked at all of them, I asked them to choose the one that seemed to most speak to them – for whatever reason. After they had chosen, I had them meditate for ten minutes on their picture. I used "Music for Zen Meditation"[269] as background and asked them to think specifically about the following questions from the list they had created in Session 1:

- Who do you say that Jesus is? Who is Christ? Who is God?
- Who is Christ to me (personally)?
- What is the Christian route to forgiveness?

The exercise went well, with a few surprises. The most gruesome crucifixion picture was chosen by the Buddhist who had expressed the most difficulty with Jesus. Another Buddhist was drawn to an Asian-style painting of a Madonna and Child. Neither at the time of the exercise or in the evaluation was she able to articulate why the picture was so meaningful. She was the only one to ask if she

---

[269] Scott, Tony, "Music for Zen Meditation." *Verve Records*, 1965.

could keep her picture, and during the evaluation she told me she keeps it hanging on the mirror in her bedroom. She said that there were no words to describe her feelings except for a radiance, almost an aura, an ethereal quality. She also mentioned that, although she had been baptized in a Lutheran church, her father had been a non-practicing Roman Catholic and her mother had been very anti-Catholic. She also has an aunt who is a nun who is very involved in ecumenism, a pioneer in Catholic/Presbyterian dialogues. She had given up Christianity and been a practicing Buddhist for seventeen years, but she felt a reclaiming of her original spiritual heritage. She quoted Thich Nat Han, "go back to your roots" and said, "I can include Christianity; I don't have to push it away."

On the Christian side, there was more discussion about the need for re-imaging Jesus/Christ, acknowledging that even with a more progressive theology/christology, we still have hymns, liturgies, and creeds with which to contend. They wanted to know about current biblical studies and were interested in books and other resources that would be helpful.

Coming back

What did you learn about yourself and your own tradition? About others?

From the Christians (about your own tradition):

- I would like more of this exploration; it's a better way to learn than reading a book.
- I moved from the constraints of institutional religion to Buddhism; it was wonderful.
- I am a Christian!
- I got more clarity about things I suspected, directions to go.

(about others):

- Meditation is wonderful!
- We were like-minded politically and socially.
- Buddhist practice seems very personal, isolated, not familial.
- There is diversity in what we have to do to find meaning.
- Coming back, I was less Christian than I was and not totally comfortable with that. I am less narrowly Christian. I see my "baggage" with new eyes.

From the Buddhists (about your own tradition):

- I haven't had a lot of exposure to other types of Buddhism. I discovered something is still missing in my spiritual practice and where to find it elsewhere.
- I had forgotten how much my Judaism still informs me.
- I have trouble with Zen.
- Some things not as well thought out as I thought (Ultimate Reality)
- We were more similar than I expected. If I had not encountered eastern religion, I would be these people.
- Impressed by Lutherans, searching for something, not just academic.

I would call the Buddhist/Christian group a success. Knowing what I know now, there are certainly things I would have done differently, such as using symbols to create a sacred space for our gatherings. I would also have been more mindful of the differences among the Buddhists and of the desire of some of them for a deeper conversation about Christianity.

In conclusion, the process did not provide me with a template for doing interfaith encounters either for my own use or to teach to others. I discovered that it is not that simple. But the methodology is sound and there are many modes, tools, and activities with which to create a group experience. However, it is indeed a "messy process" into which one must enter with a spirit of adventure.

FOR REFLECTION:

- Could you envision being part of a group like this?
- What religion would you most like to "pass over" to? Why?
- What questions would you want to be part of the group discussion?

SUGGESTED READING:

- *The Way of All the Earth* by John S. Dunne[270]

---

[270] Dunne, John S., *The Way of All the Earth*. New York: Macmillan, 1972.

Chapter 19   Getting to Know Our Neighbors

Out beyond ideas of wrongdoing and rightdoing, there is a field. I'll meet you there.
- Rumi

About halfway through the Buddhist/Christian sessions, I decided to form a second group. I realized that the Christians from the Chapel, while eager, enthusiastic participants, were all very liberal in their theological outlooks. Therefore I thought that another group might provide a more diverse response to the issues. The second group was formed at All Saints Lutheran Church in Novato, CA where I was interim pastor at the time.

All Saints is a medium-sized congregation in Marin County. Membership tends to be theologically and politically diverse, very different from the Berkeley Chapel, and I thought this would provide a good contrast. The congregation was certainly aware of my interest in interfaith dialogue and my work on this project. I had already conducted several sessions dealing with interfaith subjects during the Adult Forum on Sunday morning.

One session in particular highlighted the diversity within the group. This is a continuation of a story I began back in chapter 12 when I had invited Paul and Jan Chaffee from the Interfaith Center at the Presidio in San Francisco to meet with the adult forum. I discovered that the young man who had asked, "What about 'I am the Way, the Truth and the Life, . . " sent an email to the church council president that afternoon expressing concern about the session and about all the "interfaith stuff" we had been doing since I arrived. Later in the week, when I spoke to him about it and I explained that my doctoral project was about that very question - not giving answers, but working it through together - his response was, "Yeah, I *have* wondered about that."

What his response told me is that even the more conservative members of our congregations are struggling with these questions. When I had secured approval from the church council, I publicized my need for a group of people willing to enter into three different interfaith experiences. We would visit the International Association of Sufism[271], which is located in Novato (we went there twice), the

Brahma Kumaris,[272] who had just moved into their new retreat center in Novato, and a Soka Gakkai[273] Buddhist group. It was interesting that all of these groups were neighbors to All Saints. In fact, the church's choir director at the time is a member of the Buddhist group.

Twelve people from the church participated in the excursions, not all of them for every visit. There was no pre-arranged structure to these sessions as in the Buddhist/Christian group. We simply visited each community for a ritual and a discussion time ("passing over"). After we had made all the visits, we met at the church to talk about what they had experienced and how they had responded ("coming back"). Most found the experiences interesting and educational. There were things that had impressed them, such as the Sufi's reading of the portions of the Qur'an that talk about the Virgin Mary and the hospitality shown by the Brahma Kumaris. It was also a wonderful opportunity for them to learn about and experience their own choir director's Buddhist practice. The session we attended was held in his home, which made it an even more personal experience.

There were also things that were troubling to them. I asked them to think about what was congruent with their own beliefs and practices and what was not. Most obvious was the Lutheran view of God's grace and the fact that they did not see that present in the other traditions. Some were troubled by what they saw as "works righteousness" in the Buddhist chanting of "Namu Myoho Renge Kyo" as a way to salvation and happiness. Others were put off by the picture of the Brahma Kumaris founder as a focus of meditation. Most had trouble with the Hindu ideas of many gods and of reincarnation.

Most of the participants could identify questions or issues that these encounters raised for them, including:

- Is God just God – the same entity for all? (how does polytheism fit?)
- Works vs. Grace
- Body/Spirit duality
- Reincarnation

[271] http://ias.org
[272] http://www.brahmakumaris.org
[273] http://www.sgi.org

- Meaning of Baptism
- Forgiveness through Jesus' sacrifice on the cross
- The Trinity as God at work in the world creating community
- The role of hospitality

Obviously there was not as much time in these visits as in the nine-week Buddhist/Christian project. However, as I reflected on the experience, I realized that, even though the All Saints congregation is more diverse, the group that volunteered for the visits was also a self-selected group, people who are open to new experiences and different ways of thinking about their own religious tradition. The person who had trouble with Jan Chaffee's answer to his question was not one of the participants; his response might have been very different. It was an educational experience for the group.

The following two examples were conveyed to me almost six months after the visits, so there is some evidence that there are long-term effects. Both stories were told during a farewell event my last Sunday in the congregation. One participant talked about how his own faith had been strengthened by these encounters. He was appreciative of the opportunity to be part of the project. He had discovered that other traditions were very similar to his own in some ways, and in some ways they were very different. In his experience, even the differences were acceptable because it helped him to think about his own beliefs and be able to articulate them better.

Another participant, a seminary student, expressed appreciation from her perspective as a future church leader. According to some of her professors, the interfaith question is going to be the "next big issue" confronting the church and she was glad to have the opportunity to participate.

If I were to form a group like this again, I would hope to have more time to organize, plan, recruit and evaluate. I would have an initial orientation session, or at least provide them with some material to read and questions to take with them into the experiences. I would also build in a reflection time after each encounter. This may be the easiest kind of interfaith encounter to arrange in a congregation; therefore it would be important to tighten up the process in this setting.

FOR REFLECTION:

- Do you identify either with the person who had been raised by parents in the mission field abroad or with the one who asked the question, "What about Jesus saying 'I am the Way, the Truth and the Life , . . "? Why or why not?
- Are there religious groups in your neighborhood you have visited? If so:
  - What do you remember that seemed similar to your beliefs or practices?
  - What was different?
  - How did you feel while in the experience?
  - Did you feel any resistance within yourself?
  - As you have reflected on the experience, what resonated with you as Christian? What caused dissonance?
  - As you think about the diversity of religions and beliefs in your community, what questions are raised for you as a Christian?

SUGGGESTED READING:

- *My Neighbor's Faith* by Jennifer Howe Peace, Or N. Rose and Gregory Mobley, editors[274]

---

[274] Peace, Jennifer Howe, Or N. Rose and Gregory Mobley, editors, *My Neighbor's Faith: stories of interreligious encounter, growth, and transformation.* Maryknoll, NY: Orbis Books, 2012.

Chapter 20   Pluralism Summer I, II and III

We believe our wisdom will only be enhanced by continued conversation with all of our neighbors. Together we work for peace, justice, and the good of all people and all creation.   —from the First United Lutheran Church web site

Back in the spring of 2013, I had an idea for a series of adult forums at First United. I wanted to invite guests from different religious traditions to meet with members of the congregation. The purpose would be both to learn about another religion from an actual practitioner (passing over) and to reflect on implications for our own beliefs and practices (coming back). What actually transpired was something quite different.

As Pluralism Sunday approached, our worship planning team was discussing how we might organize these forums, but we were running into problems with timing and scheduling. Then we had the idea: why not incorporate these interfaith visits into our actual worship service? And instead of observing one Pluralism Sunday, we would have a whole summer of interfaith encounters. The only question was whether we would be able to find twelve speakers to cover the entire summer. With my contacts through the Interfaith Center at the Presidio, I was confident that we could pull it off. And we did.

We decided to give the sermon time to each speaker to present what it was that they loved about their religion or practice and to answer questions from the congregation afterwards. We also decided to ask our guests if they would like to contribute a reading, prayer, song or meditation to be included in the service. Representatives came from Buddhism, Judaism, Hinduism, Paganism, Sikhism, Baha'i, Secular Humanism, Islam and Religious Science. From the Christian tradition, we welcomed a Swedenborgian[275] minister and a Roman Catholic Woman Priest.[276] Some, but not all, submitted readings to be included. Our Baha'i speaker brought a whole contingent with him and one of the group offered a chant. The Pagan representative, an elder of the Covenant of the Goddess, led us in an earth-centered

---

[275] http://www.swedenborg.org/Home.aspx
[276] http://romancatholicwomenpriests.org

meditation. And our Hindu guest created a mandala in chalk on the sidewalk outside the church door to consecrate our time together.

As we moved through the summer, I realized that for the sake of continuity it would have been helpful to give our speakers a specific topic to address. I also recognized that I was not providing the congregation enough opportunity for "coming back" to reflection about Christianity. When we decided to hold Pluralism Summer II, I knew we would have to make some adjustments. (A lovely outcome of the first summer is that Sridevi Ramanathan, our Hindu guest, has become a good friend and helped me design the themes for Pluralism Summer II and III.)

As we prepared for the second summer of interfaith engagement, we decided on the theme of "Deeper Connections: An Interfaith Exploration of Our Relationship with the Earth." We asked each speaker to answer the question: how does your tradition inform how you think about caring for the environment. Again, we had a diverse line-up. Some of the guests were repeat performers. Others were new. We added a representative from the Brahma Kumaris,[277] who have a meditation center just a few blocks from our church. Chris Highland, a free-thinking naturalist, brought us a copy of his book, *Meditations of John Muir: Nature's Temple*.[278] Our Buddhist speaker that year was originally from the Sherpa ethnic group in Nepal, who told us about the sacredness of Mt. Everest and the ecological damage done to it by overuse by climbers.

In addition to the speakers that year, there was a provision for congregational response. Each week in our bulletin, there was a tear-off sheet with the following questions:

- What did you hear that you didn't know before?
- What did you hear that was similar to Christianity (as you understand it)?
- What did you hear that was different from your understanding?

---

[277] http://www.brahmakumaris.org
[278] Highland, Chris, *Meditations of John Muir: Nature's Temple*. Birmingham AL: Wilderness Press, 2001.

- How do <u>you</u> answer the questions: How does being a Christian inform <u>your</u> thoughts about creation care? <u>Your</u> practice?

Quite a few members of the congregations turned in their tear-sheets with thoughtful responses.

Our theme for Pluralism Summer III was gender. Speakers were invited to address questions such as:

- Is there a feminine aspect of the Divine in your tradition?
- How does your tradition reflect that aspect? Do women appear in sacred texts?
- Does your tradition inform how women should act and be?
- Are there any ways in which women have been left out? What's missing, lost or undervalued?
- What is your own story in reference to this issue?

Some of our new invitees include Reverend Masato Kawahatsu, a senior minister with the Konko[279] Churches of Northern California and Mitch Mayne, an openly gay, active Latter-day Saint (Mormon). Again, there is a tear-off sheet for congregational feedback.

During each Pluralism Summer, our liturgy also reflected our theme. I had found a Service of Holy Communion on the web site of Rex Hunt, a retired minister of the Uniting Church in Australia. His site, which offers "Sermons, Liturgies, Prayers, and Articles from a progressive/post-liberal theological perspective,"[280] included one, which we adapted to fit into our own liturgy. Here is part of the Words of Institution:

> We break this bread for the broken earth, ravaged and plundered for greed.
> **May there be healing of our beautiful blue and green planet.**
> We break this bread for our broken humanity, for the powerful and the powerless

[279] http://konkofaith.org.
[280] http://www.rexaehuntprogressive.com.

trapped by exploitation and oppression.

May there be the healing of humanity.

We break this bread for those who follow other paths: for those who follow the

noble path of the Buddha, the yogic path of the Hindus; the way of the Eternal

Guru of the Sikhs; the namelessness of the Tao, for the creation-centered indigenous religions; the Baha'i vision of unity; and for the children of Abraham

and Sarah and Hagar—the Jews and the Muslims.

May there be healing where there is pain and woundedness.[281]

Now, I can imagine many readers thinking, "But that's the San Francisco Bay Area; we could never do that here." And perhaps you couldn't or wouldn't even want to. Remember, each church must forge its own path. However, I want to tell you about another congregation, which did something similar.

Church of the Nativity, United Church of Christ, pastored by the Rev. Ruth E. Snyder, is in a suburb of Buffalo, NY. Between the 9:00 contemporary service and the 10:30 traditional service, worship attendance is around two hundred each Sunday. In 2014, a member, who was involved in the Network of Religious Communities,[282] suggested they observe Pluralism Sunday. Like First United, the worship committee responded with, "Why just one Sunday?" And they decided to hold their "Many Paths" series for one month at their 9:00 am contemporary worship service. Each guest speaker was asked to share "What I love most about my faith tradition is…" Here is the report from Pastor Snyder:

---

[281] Hunt, Rex A. E. and John W.H. Smith, *Why Weren't We Told?* Farmington, MN: Polbridge Press, 2013, 236 – 239.

[282] The Network of Religious Communities (NRC) is an interreligious/ecumenical organization of denominations, congregations, and religious organizations located in Western New York State, U.S.A. and the Niagara Peninsula of Southern Ontario, Canada. http://www.religiousnet.org

Worship attendance at the Contemporary Service in May of 2014, when we did the Many Paths series, was 52% higher than May 2013. That's huge!!! In fact, I'm pretty certain that our average attendance during that month was the highest ever for us at the Contemporary service. So, if people think folks aren't interested in this, I think this proves them wrong.

A story - just recently I was visiting with a young couple who have been coming to our church for over a year now. They are textbook Millennials in many ways -- in their mid- 20s; he was raised in a church; she was taught that religion was like Santa Clause and should be avoided at all costs; looking to raise a family. They began coming to Nativity just before that May series and were very impressed that our church was doing such a series. This was particularly valuable for her because it gave an impression of an openness she didn't believe existed in churches.

So, the series impacted new people but also our long-term members. In fact, the attendance at the traditional service dropped by an average of 30 people each week because many of those folks switched to the Contemporary service in order to hear the speakers. So, to be truthful, the figure of the 52% increase wasn't necessarily new people but people who switched services. Again, though, this indicates the level of interest in interfaith learning.

In a further conversation with Pastor Snyder, she said that, while there had not been a "coming back" component to the series, they would definitely do something like "Many Paths" again.

FOR REFLECTION:

- What is your reaction to the idea of a Pluralism Summer?
- Could you envision doing a series like Nativity, UCC did?
- How would you go about planning and inviting speakers?
- How might it be possible to get feedback from your congregation?

SUGGESTED READING:

- *The Illustrated World's Religions: A Guide to Our Wisdom Traditions* by Huston Smith[283]
- *Sourcebook of the World's Religions* by Joel Beversluis[284]

---

[283] Smith, Huston, *The Illustrated World's Religions: A Guide to Our Wisdom Traditions.* HarperOne; 1st HarperCollins Pbk. Ed edition (August 18, 1995)

[284] Beversluis, Joel, *Sourcebook of the World's Religions.* Novato, CA: New World Library, 1993.

PART VII   Joining the Parade

"build a float and join in." - Theodore Brelsford

In response to an author who described the disorienting effects of pluralism as that of the "relentless parade,"[285] Theodore Brelsford turns the negative-sounding observation into an opportunity for imagination and creativity:

"It occurs to me that one way to respond to a parade which seems relentless is to build a float and join in. One dimension of religious education in a context of pluralism might include (metaphorical) float building. In the festive context of the celebration of diversity, what should our float look like? What symbolic images might we include, and what is it that those symbols symbolize?"[286]

I tried this out at my workshop at the Parliament of the World's Religions. After an hour of telling stories and surfacing issues and questions, we began putting symbols for our float up on newsprint. It was a lively, fun exercise. Not everyone agreed on each symbol. Someone wondered if we might have to have more than one float. Unfortunately, time ran out. These conversations do take time. But I learned that Brelsford's metaphorical float idea is a good one.

And so now we turn from my story to yours. It is time to decide if you want to join the parade. If you do, then it is time to begin to construct your float. But before you do, there are some preliminary preparations to be made. In the next chapters, I will discuss:

- Safety and Pastoral care
- Leadership
- Implications for the Congregation

---

[285] Gergen, Kenneth J., *The Saturated Self: Dilemmas of Identity in Contemporary Life.* NY: Basic Books, 1991, quoted in Theodore Brelsford, "Christological Tensions in a Pluralistic Environment: Managing the Challenges of Fostering and Sustaining Both Identity and Openness," *Religious Education,* (Spring 1995): 176.

[286] Brelsford, Theodore, "Christological Tensions in a Pluralistic Environment: Managing the Challenges of Fostering and Sustaining Both Identity and Openness." *Religious Education,* 90, no2 (Spring 1995): *174-189,* 188.

Chapter 21 Safety and Pastoral Care

Oh, the comfort, the inexpressible comfort of feeling safe with a person . . .
- Dinah Craik[287]

For some people, entering into an *inter*faith experience can be confrontational. For some, engaging in *intra*faith conversation can be equally or more challenging. For this reason, I usually begin a new group with the poem, "It Is Difficult, O God" by C.S. Song (Appendix A). I do this to let them know that discomfort is to be expected, in fact it is perfectly normal.

Having said that, it is essential to create an environment of respect and safety. By safety, I do not mean that one's belief system may not be shaken. It is entirely possible that it might be. What I mean by a safe environment is one in which viewpoints are respected and in which the leader is capable of managing the group process under all circumstances. There will inevitably be challenging ideas and differences of opinion. There will often be conversations that will cause some participants to become distressed or upset. The idea is not to avoid conflict, disagreements or upset, but to manage them in appropriate and safe ways.

This is why pastoral care must also be available. Not everyone in a group will be in the same place and those places are likely to shift. Because matters of religion are deeply personal and an intimate part of our being, challenges to one's beliefs can be threatening and disturbing. Personal issues do surface. For some, passing over and/or coming back can be a bumpy ride. Some people undergo a period of deconstruction and reconstruction of their belief system and will need support in the process. The pastoral leader needs to be self-aware, compassionate and supportive. Other sensitive pastoral issues may arise as well.

Hopefully, most participants will be reassured by simply hearing that and knowing that any questions and doubts that arise are not bad signs, but a part of the natural process of discovery. Those

---

[287] Craik, Dinah, *A Life for a Life*. UK: Dodo Press, 2012. Kindle edition, location 4349.

who need further assistance or who continue to be troubled should know that they have access to a pastor or spiritual advisor who is interfaith-friendly and who can work with them.

One way of creating a space of safety and trust is setting and agreeing to ground rules for conversation. Krister Stendahl's "Three Rules for Interfaith Discussion and Religious Understanding"[288] is a good place to start:

1. If you are going to ask the question what do others believe, ask them, not their critics, not their enemies.
2. If you are going to compare, don't compare your bests with their worsts, but compare bests with bests.
3. Leave room for "holy envy" (the ability to recognize something in the other religious tradition or faith that you admire and wish, in some way, could be reflected in your own).

There are other good options available in Appendix II. Explaining and using these guidelines will set the tone for the group. Even though participants may have known one another a long time, some may hesitate to bring up questions that seem to go against the teachings of the church. Some opinions and ideas may even sound shocking – heretical, even! The leader may have to remind the group (and her/himself) of its agreement, but when participants take these issues seriously in the beginning, the groundwork has been laid for an *intra*faith encounter with transformational possibilities.

The first thing to do, of course, is to begin in prayer. I suggest also lighting a candle to remind the group of the presence of the Spirit of Pentecost, which brings courage, creativity, possibility and faith – in the midst of what appears to be chaos.

When it comes to approaching individuals or groups from other traditions, respect and safety are also crucial. When we don't already know the people we wish to invite into dialogue or have a referral from an interreligious organization, we have to understand

---

[288] Stendahl is reported to have articulated these at a 1985 press conference in Stockholm, Sweden, while he was bishop of Stockholm– in response to opposition to the building of a temple there by The Church of Jesus Christ of Latter-day Saints.

that they might be reluctant to enter into a relationship with us. Christians especially must recognize that we have a lot of history to overcome with some of our neighbors. We must establish trust. Before we can proceed with any further activity, we must be clear about our motivations. Hopefully, once we convey that our intention is not conversion, we can begin a relationship.

It is also normal for there to be some anxiety before making a contact; no one wants to do anything that would be incorrect or offensive. However there are resources available that describe the proper etiquette when visiting or participating in a worship service or ritual (see suggested reading at the end of this chapter) . It is also appropriate to ask about these issues before making the visit. For instance, when the All Saints group went to a Sufi prayer service, we received from them guidelines on appropriate dress, what we could expect to happen, and the invitation to join in or not as we felt comfortable. It is never improper to ask for such information. The important thing is to recognize the joy and the mutual benefits to be gained in such encounters and not to allow normal anxiety about new situations get in the way of getting to know our neighbors.

And, of course, when an encounter is scheduled, creating a safe space must be part of the group-building (or rather community-building) task. Planners must take into account the need for emotional safety, the recognition of fears and anxieties. Again, explaining and using "Guidelines for Conversation" or any of the other similar tools can be useful. Another way to bring a group together in a safe way is to list all the questions that participants have and hope to address together. No question or issue should be off the table, although it may not be possible to get to each and every one of them (the group may need to decide on which ones to prioritize).

I learned that entering into an exploration of other peoples' religious faith and practice is a wonder-filled experience. For me, hearing another's story is an intimate look inside that person's heart, and that is not something to be taken lightly. In both my *inter*faith and *intra*faith encounters, I have heard stories of joy, as well as stories of pain and hurt. In many of the encounters, each participant brought his or her whole self into the process. Entering into an examination of religious beliefs took us even more deeply into one another's lives. It was crucial that an atmosphere of safety and trust had been created because, as I came to realize, the ground of this kind of encounter is a place of extreme intimacy and vulnerability. It is sacred ground. I often found myself in awe at the willingness of many of the participants to give of themselves, not only in terms of time, but more importantly in terms of openness -- to me, to others, to their own growth process. It is a privilege to be in the company of such people.

FOR REFLECTION:

- Have you ever been part of a group where you felt completely safe and able to express whatever was on your mind?
- If so, how was that environment of safety established and maintained?
- Who would you go to for spiritual care if you had a question or concern raised by a discussion of *inter*faith or *intra*faith matters?

SUGGESTED READING:

- "It Is Difficult, O God" by C.S. Song (Appendix A)
- *How to Be a Perfect Stranger: A Guide to Etiquette in Other People's Religious Ceremonies, Volumes 1 and 2* by Arthur J. Magida[289]

---

[289] Magida, Arthur J., *How to Be a Perfect Stranger: A Guide to Etiquette in Other People's Religious Ceremonies, Volumes 1 and 2*. Woodstock, VT: Jewish Lights Publications, 1995-1997.

Chapter 22 Leadership

The best way of knowing the inwardness of our neighbor is to know ourselves.

-Walter Lippmann

Whether you are a pastor, a seminarian or a lay leader, facilitating an *intra*faith conversation requires more than intellectual knowledge. There is more to it than reading questions from a book and giving prescribed answers. This chapter will address the optimal characteristics of a group leader. While no one is good at everything, these will hopefully provide some guidance.

It is imperative to remember that, as stated before, people are at the heart of this work. Bringing new information and new challenges into the realm of peoples' faith can be disconcerting. Sensitivity is required. At the same time, the leader may be undergoing similar challenges. It is a very vulnerable position in which to place yourself.

For example, early on in my doctoral work, I led an *intra*faith workshop at our annual synod assembly. I began by introducing myself as a Lutheran pastor and explained my interest and experience in the subject. I also said that I was not there to give them any answers, and that in one hour we would just barely scratch the surface of our topic. One man immediately raised his hand and said, "Did you say you're a pastor?" When I replied in the affirmative he said, with an incredulous expression, "Then how can you say you don't know the answer?"

I was suddenly aware of the importance, in a setting like this, of being secure in my own identity. In that setting, I was not "preaching to the choir" but encountering not only some people who had no experience in doing any kind of interfaith thinking, but also some who came with suspicion or concerns for the orthodoxy of my presentation. In answer to the question, I backed up and reiterated that I am indeed a pastor, a Lutheran one, and that I am a Christian. I sensed some relief in the room and realized that affirming my credentials needed to be an important part of my introduction. It also affirmed the importance of self-awareness, self-identification and my own integrity as I seek to relate to others.

It is also essential to maintain a non-anxious presence in the face of challenges, fear or disagreements. For instance, the person who had expressed his incredulity that I was a pastor, raised his hand several times to ask questions about the Interfaith Center at the Presidio. I answered his questions but he did not seem satisfied with my responses. Finally, at the end of the workshop, as people were leaving, he asked me point blank whether the Interfaith Center's mission was to convert others to Christianity. When I responded in the negative, he left shaking his head. But this exclusivist kind of response is as much to be as expected as is the pluralistic view of others. An *intra*faith leader needs to be able to work with both and everything in between.

An *intra*faith leader also needs to be aware of where she or he is positioned on the continuum between exclusivism and pluralism. This doesn't mean this position will never change. It does mean that the leader is willing to observe herself/himself throughout the process and work through any issues that arise.

Anthropologist Ruth Behar, writing in her autobiographical book, *The Vulnerable Observer*, says "Nothing is stranger than this business of humans observing other humans."[290] In her discipline, which incorporates both objective data and subjective experience, she recounts how she struggled with the issue of the vulnerability of self-disclosure. This issue also arises for me in my *intra*faith work.

How much of my own story should I reveal? My own theology? My own conclusions? In search of my own answers, I have read and studied and wrestled with my own theology, christology, and biblical interpretation. I know that I have knowledge to share, but I do not want to impose my conclusions on others. I believe that it is important, especially when working with people new to interfaith thinking, to "accept them where they are" without judgment or interference in their process of discovery.

Facing the same kind of dilemma, Ruth Behar knew that inserting her personal story into her work was not the traditional way of doing anthropology. Yet there were times when it was appropriate and useful. Behar offers some good advice:

---

[290] Behar, Ruth, *The Vulnerable Observer: Anthropology that Breaks Your Heart.* Boston: Beacon Press, 1996, 5.

Vulnerability doesn't mean that anything personal goes. The exposure of the self who is also a spectator has to take us somewhere we couldn't otherwise get to. It has to be essential to the argument, not a decorative flourish, not exposure for its own sake.[291]

The vulnerability of self-disclosure, then, is appropriate as long as it is intentional. And in order for it to be intentional, one must be self-aware. "Know thyself," the ancient advice from the Oracle of Delphi, is as applicable here as anywhere. The story that I bring into my work, my history, experiences, attitudes, biases, and expectations, is important, both to this study and to any further work I do in interfaith education. How my story is incorporated into the work is an issue that is still a work in progress. The vulnerability and openness of the leader is a crucial issue that, I believe, needs to be continually addressed by each of us.

In May 2004 I was asked to be a part of the leadership for an interfaith retreat at the Wellspring Retreat Center in Philo, CA. My specific task as part of the leadership team was to address the "inner work" of interreligious encounters, to ask what we do when we "bump up" against one another's beliefs and/or practices. There were about thirty people who participated in the retreat. Some of the traditions represented were: Bah'ai, Buddhist (Zen, Tibetan and Vipassana), Jewish (religious and secular), Muslim (Sunni and Sufi), Humanist, Native American, and Christian (Roman Catholic, Episcopalian, Lutheran, Presbyterian, UCC). Some identified themselves as either Interfaith or Interfaith/Christian.

Several incidents occurred, both during and after my portion of the retreat on the second day. I had begun by playing "The Christians and the Pagans" by Dar Williams.[292] The song talks about a family Thanksgiving dinner that includes a visit from family members who are pagans. In a light-hearted way, I began to explain my intention of surfacing some of the challenges of interfaith relations. One man interrupted, however, to assert that there was no need to do this, since I was "preaching to the choir." His contention was that, by

---

[291] Ibid, 14.
[292] Williams, Dar, "The Christians and the Pagans" NY: Razor & Tie Direct, 2001.

virtue of being at the retreat, we were all "on the same page" and did not have any problems or challenges that needed to be surfaced and discussed. The group seemed to be in agreement.

At this point, in order to move the discussion forward, I decided that, in light of Ruth Behar's advice on intentional vulnerability, it would be appropriate to share a personal experience. I told the story of being at a Christian funeral with my Jewish friend and my discomfiture with the exclusive gospel text. One of the Jewish participants then became quite animated and began to talk about her experiences with Christian exclusivity. Then another woman, who had originally come from a conservative Christian background, began to cry and shared her struggle with the Christian scriptures. Even though she had intellectually rejected their exclusive claims, they were still part of her history and part of her. She recognized that on an emotional and spiritual level, they were still a powerful influence that needed to be addressed. Another participant shared that she had had a similar reaction from her background as a conservative Jew. These responses finally opened up the discussion on a deeper level. We may indeed have been an interfaith choir, but we surely did not all sing in the same key.

The session appeared to end on a down note. My initial reaction was to feel guilty for ruining the upbeat mood, but later several people confided their appreciation for raising some of the deeper personal issues of interfaith encounter and providing a forum for discussion. They agreed that it was work that needed to be done and there was much more conversation about it throughout the retreat.

Another incident actually began during my presentation, but ended later with one of the Muslim participants leaving the retreat. Her explanation, given to one of the other Muslims was, "This is not interfaith." The cause of her upset was the discussion by a few of the women who had identified themselves as lesbians. In a presentation by another of the Muslim participants, it was emphatically stated that in Islam homosexuality is not acceptable. This was clearly an example of "bumping up" against one another's beliefs, and the leadership was challenged with working through the implications.

The leadership met over dinner that evening. Some did not think we needed to do anything about what had happened, but we finally decided that the issue did need to be addressed by the whole group. For my part, I thought this was a perfect illustration of what I had been exploring in my doctoral thesis and that to ignore it would be both a loss to my project and to the integrity of our retreat community. We decided to use a group exercise the following morning in order to help the whole group discuss what had happened. Again, several participants expressed their appreciation for raising the difficult issues and for the frank discussion we were able to have.

These were incidents that happened in an *inter*faith setting, but the same dynamics may come into play in an *intra*faith group as well. Even though all the participants were very open to and looking for interfaith experiences, there was still within the group a variety of understandings and expectations of the meaning and purpose of an interfaith gathering. The dismissive comment from the man at the beginning ("You're preaching to the choir!") and the distressed response of the woman who left ("This is not interfaith!") illustrate beautifully the differing assumptions we bring to an encounter.

The reaction of the women from conservative Christian and Jewish backgrounds also reinforced my experience from the Buddhist/Christian group of the power of religious roots and the need for pastoral care to deal with experiences of this kind. While disagreements are not specifically a goal, when participants go more deeply into the encounter, differences will surface. The leader should be prepared to work with the group with creativity and imagination, presenting a non-anxious presence as a model for dealing with challenging dialogue.

An occupational hazard for clergy is to succumb to the temptation to give answers and/or impart information. Judith Berling, Professor of Chinese and Comparative Religions at the Graduate Theological Union in Berkeley, writes about the need for getting out of the way. She is writing from the standpoint of a teacher, but her wisdom is relevant to our purposes. She writes:

Empowering students means developing skills for getting out of the way. This is partially a matter of conveying in every way possible that I am also a learner; I do not have all the answers! I am not only a learner, but a co-learner with them . . . Getting out of the way also means learning to let the students take the lead (a) by listening and waiting for them to discover rather than jumping in prematurely; (b) by consistently using my authority to refer back to helpful insights and remarks by individuals or judgments by the group; (c) by entering into the conversation as an inquirer (a fellow seeker) rather than as the font of all answers.[293]

Berling also brings valuable advice for those who are not used to a collaborative learning environment. While it might appear that there is no direction involved in "getting out of the way," the reality is that such leadership does require responsibility and intentionality. Translating her recommendations from the classroom setting to an *intra*faith discussion group, these are four ways to create a collaborative experience:

1. ". . . design a structure (a ground) that balances substance (identifiable common concerns and issues) with an openness which draws students together into a collaborative learning environment.[294]

    Whatever format you're using (adult forum, off-site visits, etc.), the leader should be clear about the process, what will be involved, what participants can expect from you. While within the process, details might change and need to be adjusted, there should be an overall structure to hold it all together.

2. "setting the tone of the collaborative learning environment and seeing that it is sustained."[295] This is a very important part of *inter*faith and *intra*faith conversations. Remember the anxiety of the group that looked to me for intervention when the Lutheran pastor stated his beliefs about the Pagan's salvation (Chapter 9)? The leader must maintain a

---

[293] Berling, Judith, "Getting Out of the Way: A Strategy for Engaging Students in Collaborative Learning," *Teaching Theology & Religion*, Volume 1, Issue 1, page 33, February 1998.
[294] Ibid.
[295] Ibid.

non-anxious presence (actually I prefer "non-reactive presence), sustain the safe environment, provide spiritual care when necessary and keep personal feelings and needs out of the way.

3. "see that group learnings are noted, affirmed and underscored."[296] It is a good idea to know the hopes and expectations of participants in any *inter*faith or *intra*faith project. It will help in designing the process in terms of information and experiences you will want to provide. Then, periodically, you can check in with the group to make sure that those interests are being addressed.

4. "provide detailed, generous, written feedback . . ."[297] While there is usually no need for written feedback in a congregational setting, verbal comments to individuals might include, for example, affirmation of a participant's contribution to the group or acknowledgement of another's struggle with a particular concept. To the group as a whole, feedback might be a word of reassurance as they grapple with new information or a word of challenge to go further in depth with one another.

---

[296] Ibid.
[297] Ibid.

FOR REFLECTION:

- Would you be willing to organize an *inter*faith experience for your congregation? Why or why not?
- Would you be willing to lead an *intra*faith discussion? Why or why not?
- Can you identify where you are in the spectrum of interfaith theology?
  Has your position ever changed? Do you feel 'settled' in your position?
- How would you handle theological (or even "heretical") disagreements among church members?

SUGGESTED READING:

- "Getting Out of the Way: A Strategy for Engaging Students in Collaborative Learning" by Judith A. Berling. *Teaching Theology & Religion*, Volume 1, Issue 1, pages 31–35, February 1998. Available through Wiley Online Library:
  http://onlinelibrary.wiley.com/doi/10.1111/1467-9647.00006/pdf [298]

---

[298] Ibid.

Chapter 23   Implications in the Congregation

Is there some other way to understand these Jesus stories and the doctrines that are said to have been based on them? - John Shelby Spong

When we take *inter*faith and *intra*faith work seriously, we will recognize that there are components of our Christian tradition that are problematic. There are also implications for our worship: prayers, hymns, liturgies, etc. The first step is becoming aware of these complications. The following are some of the categories in which they might show up.

Scripture

There are passages that do imply an exclusivistic understanding of Christianity, and it is my belief that we must take them seriously and not simply ignore them. When these come up in the lectionary or in Bible studies, congregational leaders should be prepared to address the issues involved. While I have found that it is not always possible or desirable to preach a sermon on a particular problematic text, I do try to provide an introduction to the reading that gives some perspective. For example, John 14: 6 - "I am the way, and the truth, and the life. No one comes to the Father except through me."

The commentary, *Preaching the Gospels without Blaming the Jews: A Lectionary Commentary*, tackles the problem head-on.

> This text constitutes (builds up, affirms) the synagogue of Jesus' followers by its interpretation of the trustworthiness of the path to God through Jesus. Yet no amount of theological juggling in the name of particularism, a "hidden Christ," or sensitivity to John's pastoral situation, can excise the exclusivism of v. 6. However, one of John's own insights prophetically critiques this exclusivism. If God's love of the *kosmos* (3:16) is truly unconditional, then the divine love cannot be limited to Jesus' followers. Such a broad interpretation is consistent with the best insights of the First Testament that portray the God of Israel showing love and compassion for all, even Gentiles and enemies.[299]

A more pluralistic stance is taken by commentator Bruce Epperly:

> Jesus is the way to salvation in an inclusive way. All
> paths of salvation and enlighten-ment are grounded in
> the graceful energy of God. We walk the pathway to
> many mansions in many diverse ways, lured forward
> by God's moment to moment inspiration. We can still
> speak of Jesus as supreme without denigrating other
> faiths and casting doubt on peoples' eternal destinies.
> We can understand Jesus' pathway as an embracing
> grace that animates and empowers all authentic paths.
> We can be confessional pluralists, recognizing that the
> diversity of spiritual paths is not a fall from grace, but
> a reflection of God's personal relationship with every
> culture and person. Christ is the way that includes all
> authentic ways, enabling all ways to be fruitful.[300]

The introduction I used for the Fifth Sunday of Easter in 2014
was also adapted from Epperley's *Adventurous Lectionary*:

> Today's gospel could be described as 'three promises
> and a problem.' The problem emerges in verse 6: 'I am
> the way and the truth and the life . . . ,' which can be
> destructive if taken out of the context of John's Gospel
> and a holistic understanding of Jesus' life and message.
> When we interpret John 14:6 imaginatively and
> inclusively, then it becomes our fourth promise: God
> guides us on the pathway wherever we are on our

---

[299] Allen, Ronald J. and Clark M. Williamson, *Preaching the Gospels without Blaming the Jews: A Lectionary Commentary*. Louisville, KY: Westminster John Knox Press, c2004, 43.

[300] Epperly, Bruce. "The Adventurous Lectionary: The Fifth Sunday of Easter – May 18, 2014." patheos.com.
http://www.patheos.com/blogs/livingaholyadventure/2014/05/the-adventurous-lectionary-the-fifth-sunday-of-easter-may-18-2014/_(accessed February 26, 2016).

journey; God's energy enlightens all persons in all cultures; makes a way where there is no way; and leads all creation in all of its diversity to wholeness.[301]

There are other resources for rethinking how these passages are presented. It may take some extra time and creativity, but this is an important way of aligning a pluralistic theology with traditional scriptures.

Other scripture passages, however, are not so "redeemable." One of the problems with John's gospel is the characterization of the Jews. While some people know that this latest of the four gospels reflected the growing split between Judaism and the followers of Jesus, not all will understand the context. In *The Passion According to John*, which is often read on Good Friday, the phrase "the Jews" appears nineteen times in the *New Revised Standard Version* (NRSV). We do not have to look very far for evidence of the damage done by anti-Jewish rhetoric. Language matters. Repetition nineteen times only reinforces hateful stereotypes.

In *The Inclusive Bible* (TIB),[302] "the Jews" appears only six times, when the reference is to the title "King of the Jews." In seven places, "Temple authorities" is used to convey the part played by Jewish leadership is the crucifixion of Jesus. In other places "the Jews" is omitted entirely. For example, in contrast to John 19:20 in the NRSV, which reads *"Many of the Jews read this inscription,"* TIB has *"Many of the people* read this inscription." And in verse 21, where the NRSV reads: *"the chief priests of the Jews* said to Pilate, 'Do not write, "The King of the Jews . . . ",* TIB has: *The chief priests* said to Pilate, "Don't write 'King of the Jews . . . '"*.

Another example of eliminating anti-Semitic is changing John 7: 1 from "After this Jesus went about in Galilee. He did not wish to

[301] Epperly, Bruce. "The Adventurous Lectionary: The Fifth Sunday of Easter – May 18, 2014." patheos.com.

http://www.patheos.com/blogs/livingaholyadventure/2014/05/the-adventurous-lectionary-the-fifth-sunday-of-easter-may-18-2014/ (accessed February 28, 2016).

[302] *The Inclusive Bible.*

go about in Judea because *the Jews* were looking for an opportunity to kill him." (NRSV) to "After this, Jesus walked through Galilee. He had decided not to travel to Judea, because *the Temple authorities* were trying to kill him." (TIB)

And another: changing John 20:19 from "When it was evening on that day, the first day of the week, and the doors of the house where the disciples had met were locked for fear of *the Jews* . . ." (NRSV) to "In the evening of that same day, the first day of the week, the doors were locked in the room where the disciples were, for fear of the *Temple authorities* . . ." (TIB)

Two other good practical resources that I discovered while writing this book are a website and a book. The website is called *Sermons without Prejudice*[303] by Richard K. Taylor and David P. Efroymson, Ph.D. Its stated purpose is "to counter this anti-Semitism by addressing the anti-Judaism that some New Testament readings may convey." The book is *Preaching the Gospels without Blaming the Jews: A Lectionary Commentary*[304] by Ronald J Allen and Clark M. Williamson. These would be excellent places to start.

Prayers

While scripture texts are places where exclusivity issues often arise, there are other occasions when thoughtfulness and sensitivity is required. A prime example is the Bidding Prayer[305] that is traditionally used on Good Friday. We have thankfully advanced beyond this version of the petition "For the Jewish people":

> Let us pray also for the faithless Jews: that Almighty God may remove the veil from their hearts; so that they too may acknowledge Jesus Christ our Lord.

> Almighty and eternal God, who dost not exclude from thy mercy even Jewish faithlessness: hear our prayers, which we offer for the blindness of that people; that acknowledging the light of thy Truth, which is Christ, they may be delivered from their darkness.

---

[303] http://www.sermonswithoutprejudice.org.
[304] Allen, Ronald J and Clark M. Williamson,.
[305] Also called "prayers of intercession" or "prayers of the people"

Through the same our Lord Jesus Christ, who liveth and reigneth with thee in the unity of the Holy Spirit, God, forever and ever. Amen.[306]

More contemporary versions soften the language and include others:

For the Jewish people

Let us pray for the Jewish people, to whom God spoke through the prophets, that they will acknowledge Jesus as the Christ foretold by the prophets.

Almighty Father, long ago you gave your promise to Abraham and his descendants. Grant that your chosen people may share with us the fullness of your redemption.

For those who do not yet believe in Christ

Let us pray for all who do not yet believe in Jesus Christ, that the light of the Holy Spirit will show them the way of salvation.

Heavenly Father, remember those who do not remember you. Have mercy on those who have rejected your grace. Guide those who seek to make sense of their lives, so that they may find their salvation in Jesus Christ.[307]

---

[306] *Roman Missal*, 1920 typical edition, 221-222.

[307] "Good Friday Bidding Prayer." cowadmin.s3.amazonaws.com/.../wp.../Bidding-Prayer-Good-Friday.doc (this document is cached. If you look for 'Good Friday Bidding Prayer" on Google you can download it.)

Another version simply includes all non-Christians:

> Let us pray for all who are outside the Church, that our Lord God would be pleased to deliver them from their error, call them to faith in the true and living God and His only Son, Jesus Christ, our Lord, and gather them into His family, the Church: Almighty and everlasting God, because You seek not the death but the life of all, hear our prayers for all who have no right knowledge of You, free them from their error, and for the glory of Your name bring them into the fellowship of Your holy Church; through Jesus Christ, our Lord."[308]

Even this much more moderate version from the Evangelical Lutheran Church (ELCA) could be interpreted in several ways:

> Let us pray for the Jewish people, the first to hear the word of God.
>
> Almighty and eternal God, long ago you gave your promise to Abraham and your teaching to Moses. Hear our prayers that the people you called and elected as your own may receive the fulfillment of the covenant's promises. We ask this through Christ our Lord.[309]

While a definite improvement in language and tone, it seems to me that the authors have created an ambiguous prayer. Are we affirming the covenant God made with Abraham (and Sarah, by the way)? Or is it praying for the conversion of the Jews? Given the history of Christian anti-Semitism, serious thought should be given to including it in the very service which remembers the death of Jesus.

---

[308] Commission on Worship of the Lutheran Church--Missouri Synod, *Lutheran Service Book: Altar Book*. St. Louis, MO: Concordia Publishing House, c2006.406ff.

[309] *Evangelical Lutheran Worship Leader's Edition*. Mpls: Augsburg Fortress, 2006, pp.636-638.

Hymns

I wrote about "I Am the Bread of Life" back in Chapter Two. But there are other beloved hymns that may cause you to raise an eyebrow if you have been involved in *inter*faith and *intra*faith thinking. For example:

All Hail the Power of Jesus' Name
Let every kindred, every tribe
on this terrestrial ball;
To him all majesty ascribe
and crown him Lord of all.

Sent Forth by God's Blessing
Sent forth by God's blessing,
Our true faith confessing . . .

You Are the Way
You are the truth;
Your word alone true wisdom can impart.
You only can inform the mind
And purify the heart.

Lift High the Cross
Lift high the cross,
the love of Christ proclaim;
Till all the world adores his sacred name

I am not recommending that we all discontinue singing these hymns (although personally I cannot envision ever again using "I Am the Bread of Life" or "You Are the Way" in worship; there is just way too much baggage). What I do suggest is that, as you become sensitized to exclusive language in our worship service material, it will become part of your *intra*faith conversation. At that point, it will also be necessary to include clergy and worship planners.

As you can imagine, sensitivity is again required. This is true for all of these matters that pertain to worship planning.

FOR REFLECTION:

- How does changing "the Jews" to the Temple authorities in John's Passion account change the meaning of the story? Is this a good or a bad thing? Why?

- How do you interpret the Good Friday Bidding Prayer from the ELCA? Does it
affirm the covenant God made with Abraham and Sarah? Or does it pray for the
conversion of the Jews?
Can you think of words from other hymns or contemporary Christian songs that sound exclusive in relation to other religions?

- How would you bring the *intra*faith conversation into your congregation's worship planning process?

SUGGESTED READING:

- *The Inclusive Bible: The First Egalitarian Translation* by Priests for Equality[310]

- "Sermons without Prejudice: How to Avoid Anti-Judaism in Readings from the Church's Lectionary"[311]

---

[310] The Inclusive Bible.

[311] "Sermons without Prejudice: How to Avoid Anti-Judaism in Readings from the Church's Lectionary." sermonswithuotprejudice.org.
http://www.sermonswithoutprejudice.org (accesses February 26, 2016).

PART VIII Building Your Float

The journey of a thousand miles begins with one step. - *Lao Tzu*

So you've decided to venture into the *inter*faith/*intra*faith waters. Fantastic! The following chapters will offer you tips on when to begin, some easily do-able projects and more long-term ideas for creating your own unique float.

Chapter 24 Timing Is Everything

Start where you are. Use what you have. Do what you can. - *Arthur Ashe*

Some times might be better than others for introducing an *inter*faith/*intra*faith component in a congregation. This chapter will explore opportunities to introduce the conversation in a non-threatening way.

Your community may already be holding *inter*faith events in which your congregation could participate. Thanksgiving is one time when diverse people can find common ground. It is not a religious holiday, so people of all faiths and no faith can come together in a spirit of gratitude. If your community has such an event, encourage congregational members to attend and perhaps even participate. If your church is large enough to hold such a service, you could even offer to host in the future.

You might be asked some questions about this. Some in the congregation might question the reason for becoming involved. That is to be expected, and the non-reactive, response is best. Having a well thought out proposal for the church leadership and their buy-in for your participation will set the foundation for further involvement.

Other opportunities might come at sacred times in other religions. You might be invited to a Passover Seder or a Ramadan *iftar* (fast-breaking dinner). Some Muslim communities extend iftar invitations to those of other faiths in a spirit of hospitality. At the iftar I attended last year, along with our Muslim hosts in their home, there were three other Muslim guests, a Jewish rabbi and two Christians. We had a lively discussion about traditions in all three of the Abrahamic religions! Next week, a group from the congregation is going to another iftar. When I brought up the idea of attending, the response was quick and enthusiastic. Many people welcome an opportunity to engage in a "passing over" experience. They may not feel comfortable attending on their own, and will appreciate this way of dipping their toes into interfaith engagement. This is also a great way of introducing the *intra*faith conversation. You could go to a café afterwards to debrief the experience or make it part of the Sunday adult forum.

It would be very helpful if your community has an active

*inter*faith or *inter*religious council. You can easily find out by doing a Google search for your area. You can also find an alphabetical list of such organizations for each state on the website of the *Journal of Inter-Religious Studies*.[312] You can discover what is being done in your area and how your congregation might become involved. In my congregation's weekly newsletter, we include upcoming events listed on the calendar of the Interfaith Center at the Presidio. In fact, we have an "Interfaith News" page, in which we include news articles of interest as well as a calendar of religious holidays of the world's religions.

Again, why are you doing this? You will need to be ready to answer the question of why, for example, there is an invitation to a Ramadan *iftar* (fast-breaking dinner) in your newsletter. I am sure you can see how the *intra*faith conversation will become important.

Another perfect time to introduce an *inter*faith component into congregational life is Pluralism Sunday. I have already written about this back in Chapter 12, and you can explore the information on their web site. We have done various things in our congregation. The first year, we based our service on the theme of the Golden Rule. The Scarboro Missions web site[313] is a wonderful place to find information about using the Golden Rule as an *inter*faith resource. For many people, new to *inter*faith matters, the various texts of this same ethic across religious lines may be an informative and non-threatening introduction. Beyond that, the Pluralism Sunday web site has a growing list of things that congregations have done or plan to do, so you can find ideas there or come up with your own.

But again, I refer you back to the story in Chapter 12 in which a member of my congregation wanted to know exactly what "pluralism" meant, so he could decide whether or not he could support Pluralism Sunday. Questions such as this bring about the opportunity for *intra*faith reflection and conversation.

One of my favorite times to think about *inter*faith is Epiphany. For me, the story of the magi in Matthew's gospel is a "passing over

---

[312] "Dialogue in the United States." irdialogue.org.
http://irdialogue.org/resources/dialogue-in-us/ (accessed February 26, 2016).
[313] "The Golden Rule." scarboromissions.ca.
https://www.scarboromissions.ca/Golden_rule/index.php (accessed February 26, 2016).

and coming back" tale. These visitors, who I like to believe Matthew would have envisioned as Zoroastrian priests, crossed over into Judaism in order to honor a sacred moment in that religion.[314]

In fact, a non-canonical text from the sixth century, *The Arabic Infancy Gospel of the Savior*, tells the story this way:

> And it came to pass, when the Lord Jesus was born at Bethlehem of Judaea, in the time of King Herod, behold, magi came from the east to Jerusalem, as Zeraduscht* had predicted; and there were with them gifts, gold, and frankincense, and myrrh. And they adored Him, and presented to Him their gifts. Then the Lady Mary took one of the swaddling-bands, and, on account of the smallness of her means, gave it to them; and they received it from her with the greatest marks of honour. And in the same hour there appeared to them an angel in the form of that star which had before guided them on their journey; and they went away, following the guidance of its light, until they arrived in their own country.
>
> *Zeraduscht is a form of Zarathushtra, the founding Prophet of Zoroastrianism.[315]

They came; they honored; they returned to their own home and their own religion. I imagine a version of the story, in which these Zoroastrian holy men brought back learnings and insights about Judaism that became part of their own practice. But I also imagine an

[314] "These strangers from the Far East . . . were not idolaters, their form of worship being viewed with more tolerance and sympathy than that of other Gentiles. They were starwatchers, reading in them the destinies of the nations, whether deriving them from Balaam's prophecy (Numbers 24:17), received from Diaspora Jews, or from traditions parallel to the Old Testament, or from predictions of their own prophet Zoroaster." *The New Smith's Bible Dictionary*. s.v. "magi." Garden City, NY: Doubleday, 1966, 222.

[315] Roberts, Alexander and James Donaldson, editors, *The Ante-Nicene Fathers: Translations of the Writings of the Fathers Down to A.D. 325*, Grand Rapids, MI: W.B. Eerdmanns, 1985-1987, *406*.

*intra*faith discussion on the way home. "I agree with this." "But what about that?" "How does that fit in with what Zoroaster teaches?" These magi might help us to follow the star of Wisdom into our own *intra*faith journeys.

Other times that might be opportunities to introduce an *inter*faith theme are the Sundays when certain texts appear in the lectionary (if your church does not follow a lectionary, you can choose these passages any time). Of course, there is the Christian version of the Golden Rule: "Therefore treat others as you would have them treat you. This is the whole meaning of the Law and the prophets." - Matthew 7:12. Actually this text does not appear in the Revised Common Lectionary; Luke's version appears on All Saints Sunday, but does not include Matthew's second line "This is the whole meaning of the Law and the prophets."

This might be a good time for lectionary preachers to go off the ranch and venture into a sermon on Matthew's version (maybe Pluralism Sunday!)

Another *inter*faith-friendly text would be the Great Commandment. In Mark 12:28–31 Jesus responds to a religious scholar who had asked him to name the greatest commandment. Jesus said:

> This is the foremost: 'Hear, O Israel, God, our God, is one. You must love the Most High God with all your heart, with all your soul, with all your mind and with all your strength.' The second is this: 'You must love your neighbor as yourself.' There is no commandment greater than these.

Others would include the story of Peter and Cornelius in Acts 10, especially verses 34-35:

> So Peter said to them, "I begin to see how true it is that God shows no partiality—rather, that any person of any nationality who fears God and does what is right is acceptable to God.

and I John verse 16:

> Beloved, let us love one another because love is of
> God; everyone who loves is begotten of God and has
> knowledge of God.

Just as we should take seriously those texts that would seem to be exclusionary, we should also be willing to grapple with those that would suggest an inclusive interpretation.

However, not every congregation is ready to hear an *inter*faith theme from the pulpit. I have heard a number of speakers answer the question usually raised by clergy after a seminar on progressive Christianity: "How can I bring this stuff to my congregation?" Their answer is that they should not begin with preaching. An adult forum or book study is a much more appropriate starting place. The same answer applies to *inter*faith and *intra*faith matters. A small group is also a place to better gauge where individuals are in their thinking and in their willingness to explore new ideas.

I have learned one important lesson: never underestimate people. Years ago in Buffalo, NY, in my first foray into an adult discussion group on progressive Christianity, a study of Marcus Borg's *Meeting Jesus Again for the First Time*,[316] I was struck by the differing responses from participants. While some struggled with the material, one elderly woman came up to me after a session and exclaimed, "I wish I had read this seventy years ago!" Until that book discussion group, I had no idea that she – and others – would be so receptive.

Later, that same group was the one that decided to study the world's religions and invite guests from other traditions. It would also be the catalyst for Elsie's *intra*faith dilemma (see Introduction) and my own journey into this adventure. My advice is: watch out! You never know what that wild, creative Spirit is going to do!

Ironically, it was the September 11, 2001 attacks on New York City and Washington, DC that engendered that study. As horrific as that was, the *inter*faith community stepped up in the aftermath. Interfaith services were held in New York City and across the

---

[316] Borg, *Meeting Jesus Again for the First Time*.

country. In Buffalo, several mosques held open house and invited the community to visit and learn about them.

Ten years later, the San Francisco Opera's annual free Opera in the Park concert included an observance commemorating the tenth anniversary. It began with a "Procession of Faiths" made up of representatives from the world's religions, accompanied by Mozart's "March of the Priests."[317] Then, *inter*faith speakers joined political and civic dignitaries on stage to offer remarks and readings for the day of remembrance.

Another example of a positive *inter*faith response in a time of crisis is the San Francisco Interfaith Council. In October 1989, when the Loma Prieta earthquake rocked the Bay Area, the mayor of San Francisco asked a group of clergy and lay leaders to help provide relief for people who had lost their homes in the quake. This group had been called upon before to provide shelter for the city's homeless population. As a result of these two crises, leaders decided that it was time to form an organization that would enable the diverse religious community to work together for the good of the city.

I mention these because they are examples of *inter*faith cooperation that came about as a result of timing. Even when the precipitating event was a tragedy, people of good will chose to "seize the day" and make something good come about. The same might be true for you. For some congregations, an *inter*faith marriage in the church community might bring about a timely *intra*faith opportunity. When the college student comes home for Christmas break and declares that she is now a Wiccan would be an opportune time to open up an *intra*faith conversation. These are not outlandish examples. As church leaders and members, how ready are you to address them?

---

[317] Mozart, Wolfgang Amadeus. "March of the Priests," from *The Magic Flute*, 1791.

FOR REFLECTION:

- Do you know if your community has any interfaith events, such as a Thanksgiving service? How could you find out?
- Is there an interfaith or interreligious organization in your area? What kinds of things does it do? How is or how might your congregation be involved?
- What time or season could you envision for introducing an *inter*faith/*intra*faith component to your congregation?

  How ready do you think you are to address the *intra*faith questions that could arise at unexpected times?

SUGGESTED READING:

- *Golden Rule Chronology* by Harry J. Gensler[318]

SUGGESTED VIEWING:

- Interfaith Thanksgiving Service, Rothko Chapel Houston[319]

---

[318] Gensler, Harry, S.J. "Golden Rule Chronology." harryhiker.com. http://www.harryhiker.com/chronology.htm (accessed February 26, 2016).

319 "Interfaith Thanksgiving Service" rothkochapel.org. http://www.rothkochapel.org/index.php?option=com_content&view=article&id=129%3Ainterfaith-thanksgiving&Itemid=44 (accessed February 26, 2016).

Chapter 25   Reaching Out/ Reaching In

I believe that sharing our stories is the mot important thing we can do to get to know one another. – Zeenat Rahman[320]

Reaching Out

My first piece of advice for a congregation or a group within the congregation is simply to decide to do something. Every congregation has the opportunity to reach out to another tradition in its community in some way. It also has the ability to reach in and engage members in reflection on those opportunities.

Reaching out could be as simple as organizing a visit to the neighboring temple, mosque, or whatever group happens to be nearby. Confirmation classes are naturals for such events, and adults could be included. Depending on your context, it might even be fun to have an intergenerational follow-up discussion and see how perspectives vary among different age groups. In order to prepare for the visit (and ease some of the anxiety of entering an unknown space), the group could use any number of the books, study guides and videos available. A really good resource is Arthur, J. Magida's *How to Be a Perfect Stranger: A Guide to Etiquette in Other People's Religious Ceremonies.*[321] Another is JW Windland's "Guidelines For Arranging Group Visits To Houses Of Worship"[322]

If you don't know anything about the place you've identified for a possible visit, it would also be wise to do some research beforehand. Just as not every Christian church would be a good choice for an interfaith guest, so also not every mosque, synagogue, etc. would be ideal either. This is not to say that a neighborly

---

[320] Peace, Jennifer Howe, Or N. Rose, and Gregory Mobley, editors, *My Neighbor's Faith: stories of interreligious encounter, growth, and transformation.* Maryknoll, NY: Orbis Books, 2012, 19.

[321] Magida, Arthur, J. *How to Be a Perfect Stranger: A Guide to Etiquette in Other People's Religious Ceremonies Vol. 1 and Vol. 2,* Woodstock, VT: Jewish Lights Publications, 1995-1997.

[322] Windland, J.W. "Guidelines For Arranging Group Visits To Houses Of Worship." http://www.scarboromissions.ca/interfaith-dialogue/principles-and-guidelines-for-interfaith-dialogue/guidelines-for-arranging-group-visits-to-houses-of-worship (accessed February 24, 2016).

approach should not be made, simply to be aware that not all groups are interested in interfaith exchanges.

Reaching out could also take the form of inviting a group from another tradition to visit your congregation. Be aware, however, that some might view your invitation with some suspicion. If they do not know you, they may have concerns that you have an "agenda," such as proselytizing and hopefully converting them. Unfortunately Christianity has some negative baggage to overcome. You should be clear about your own motivations for doing something like this; if your goal is conversion, you should not be doing it. You should be able to explain to possible guests exactly what you are planning and what you expect from them. Your first priority is to offer a hospitable welcome and to put your guests at ease.

You may even have people of other faiths within your church community. If you have interfaith couples, would the non-Christian partner be willing to share his or her story? If a young person has been exploring another tradition, would she or he talk about that? If some members have friends, neighbors or coworkers of different religions, could they invite them to be part of a church interfaith event?

You might also consider hosting an interfaith speaker series. This would create a more neutral space than the worship service. Again, you want to know who your speakers are and how interfaith-friendly they are. Asking interreligious councils and organizations is a good way to get referrals for good presenters. Remember, too, that any speaker can share only from her or his own perspective. I always have to laugh when I am asked to be the Christian representative on a panel or in a discussion. Christianity has such a broad range of expressions; in no way can I claim to speak, for instance, for the Orthodox Church or the Southern Baptists. The most important thing I have to offer is my own story. The same is true for anyone asked to participate as a member of a particular tradition. There are many branches of Buddhism, for example. What you hear from one Buddhist to another may vary as widely as what you would hear from a Roman Catholic and a Christian Scientist.

A congregation that is feeling a little bolder could even offer to help plan a joint Thanksgiving service with their interfaith neighbors, if one does not already exist. From there, perhaps it could extend an invitation to a dialogue process. Ultimately, an in-depth encounter and dialogue might provide an opportunity for both groups to experience the process of "passing over and coming back." The first step is to ask, "Who is my neighbor?" and then reach out.

Reaching In

The second step, then, is to reach in. This may actually be the more challenging part. Questions may not immediately surface. Not everyone will feel the need to go more deeply into their beliefs. The challenge to "do theology" may be a hard sell. I have also discovered that not everyone has experienced the kind of crisis of Christology that I did. I was talking about this with a friend, who attributes her pluralistic theology to the pastor of the church in which she was raised.

The Rev. Dr. Ralph W. Loew served Holy Trinity Lutheran Church in Buffalo, NY from 1944 to 1975. Among the many ways he contributed to the community's civic and religious life, was as one of the organizers of Buffalo Area Metropolitan Ministries (BAMM). BAMM was founded in 1976 in order to focus on "establishing and intensifying interreligious dialogue, study and understanding."[323] So my friend fondly remembers, for example, visiting non-Christian places of worship as part of her Confirmation education. I have no doubt that being steeped in an atmosphere of mutual respect and dialogue – in a Christian context – contributed to the Christology she holds to today.

I know other faithful, thoughtful Christians who do not struggle with these issues. However, I still believe that it is important for such church leaders and members to be aware of the questions that others do raise. How <u>do</u> they answer the "Elsies" of their congregations? How <u>do</u> they deal with the "I am the Way, the Truth and the Life" challenges? An interesting *intra*faith discussion group would be comprised of both kinds of people. In such a "reaching in" practice, each would learn from the other, as well as hopefully also learning more about themselves.

---

[323] In 1999, BAMM and the Buffalo Area Council of Churches merged to form The Network of Religious Communities.

Getting such a productive discourse going might require the leader to help participants enter into the discussion. In an article entitled "The Catholic-Jewish Colloquium: An Experiment in Interreligious Learning," Mary Boys and Sara Lee offer good advice, which I have found to be of immense help. They describe the beginning of their project very simply: "We often spent hours of planning time trying to fashion just the right question." [324]

I do not always hit the mark, but I try to ask questions that do not set up any expectations of a "the right answer" but allow the group to enter into a lively conversation. When a group from my congregation attended a Ramadan fast-breaking dinner (iftar), I followed up with an email questionnaire that asked:

- What was your overall impression of the iftar experience?
- What resonated with you on a personal, spiritual level, if anything?
- What did not, if anything?
- Was there anything that was similar to Christianity, as you understand it?
- Was there anything different from Christianity, as you understand it?
- Any other comments or questions?

The questions worked. Responses were thoughtful and expressed more than the usual "everything was great." One of the themes, along with the desire to do more such events, was the similarity of the Muslim Ramadan fast to the Christian practice of fasting during Lent. As one responder, who had decided to fast that day in order to more fully experience the iftar, said:

"The similarities between the month of Ramadan and

---

[324] Boys, Mary C.; Lee, Sara S., "The Catholic-Jewish Colloquium: An Experiment in Interreligious Learning," *Religious Education*, v91 n4 p421-66 Fall 1996, 435.

the season of Lent are undeniable. Both are a time of fasting. Each a period of reflection and resisting temptation. The fasting was enlightening. I thought of food regularly throughout the day. I tried to take the chance to think of God and the idea of doing this for 30 days straight whenever I felt the urge to eat. It made me think of how many times I, and others I know, have failed to even observe my self-imposed Lenten fasting."

Two other responders also reflected:

"Fasting is an ancient Christian practice that has seemed to disappear over centuries. I think the level of devotion is stronger in Islam than that practiced among the mainstream of Christians."

"It seems that for Islam, the marking of this season is much more widespread than it is in Christianity for Lent."

Now, as part of our ongoing *intra*faith awareness, the subject of fasting will be ideal for us to take up again in Lent.

Although physically participating in a reaching out activity (such as an iftar) is ideal, the reaching in process actually could even begin before one can be planned. If you are in a location where it is more difficult to arrange interfaith encounters, you could start with a session that might set the stage for further exploration.

In a workshop I led at our synod assembly, after describing the new diverse religious America in which I live, I asked participants to divide into pairs and tell each other about an interfaith experience they had had. There was some brief confusion until we determined that, for some, "interfaith" might mean ecumenical, that is pertaining to cooperation among just Christian churches. For instance, a few Lutherans were still working on their relationships with Roman Catholicism. When we reconvened I asked the whole group to call out what issues had been raised in their various experiences. If you have a small group, you do not have to divide up. But I do find that some of the more shy folks seem to open up more quickly one on one than in a larger group.

I did discover, in the synod workshop, that the *intra*faith questions were raised immediately. The very first person who raised his hand asked: What about "I am the Way, the Truth and the Life"? I saw many heads nodding. Other issues included:

- Christian education - how do we teach our children about other faiths without confusing them?
- Implications for evangelization and mission
- Offensiveness of proselytizing
- Danger of conversion
- Interfaith families

There was, of course, far too little time to go into these in any depth. I did go over – very quickly – some information about the exclusive, inclusive and pluralist ways of approaching these questions. I then had them gather again in smaller groups to discuss:

- In which position do you think you fit? Why?
- How does your position fit and/or challenge your beliefs as a Christian?

In the reporting-back time I took a poll to see how they had responded. I was very clear in explaining that there was no right or wrong answer, no hierarchy of positions, no expectation that they should be moving from one position to another. I also told them that they did not have to raise their hands if they did not choose to do so.

The group seemed to be fairly evenly divided. Everyone appeared to participate and they did not seem to be intimidated or shy about declaring their perspective. Some expressed their indecision between one position and another: "I thought I was a pluralist, but this perennial philosophy is looking awfully good!" Others had no doubts: "I'm an exclusivist." They were clearly engaged by the material and giving it serious thought, not just as an academic exercise but in response to their own beliefs and questions. In the responses from the session, I got everything from warnings ("Be careful! People might convert") to appreciation ("I'm so glad I don't have to be exclusive to be Christian."). This is the gamut of thought within our congregations. When I conducted the same kind of process in my own congregation, one member articulated his struggle by saying, "My head tells me I'm an inclusivist; my heart says I'm an exclusivist."

This is why I wrote this book. I hope that it can be a guide for others to work through this subject – which is of great interest to people – in the context of their own congregation, in a safe environment, with good spiritual care available to them. And when reaching out is joined together with reaching in, it can be a transformative spiritual adventure.

FOR REFLECTION:

- Who are your closest interfaith neighbors? What do you know about them? What do they know about you?
- Who do you know in your wider circles who belong to a different tradition?
- What is one activity or event you could envision as a way to reach out?
- Do you have any "role models" of *inter*faith dialogue, study and understanding? If so, how did they affect your understanding of Christianity?

SUGGESTED READING:

- *Not Without My Neighbour: Issues in Interfaith Relations* by S. Wesley Ariarajah[325]

---

[325] Ariarajah, S. Wesley, *Not Without My Neighbour: Issues in Interfaith Relations.* World Council of Churches, 1999.

Chapter 26   Dreams and Visions

Your old shall dream dreams and your young shall see visions. - Joel 2: 28

While I certainly recognize that there are many things that are of concern to pastors and congregations today, I believe that *inter*faith and *intra*faith issues are not simply add-ons to a list of interesting topics. Despite the surge in interfaith interest after 9/11, not everyone is convinced of the necessity of going beyond the obligatory survey class. Often, when I am at a clergy gathering and I am asked about my doctoral work, the response I hear is, "That's interesting, but we're dealing with a lot of other issues right now in our congregation." These issues are usually issues of survival as the church seeks to find its place in today's culture. My response is that I am not interested in mere survival for the church. I am certainly aware of the survival issues. After all I am the pastor of a small congregation! But if survival is our only motivation, if we ignore the places to which God is calling us in this day and time, perhaps we should not survive.

The Elsies in our pews are asking the *intra*faith questions. Young people are asking the *intra*faith questions, and, in my observation, they are not very interested in a church that does not address them. If a congregation is serious about being a relevant part of life in the 21st century, *inter*faith awareness and encounter must be an integral part of its mission statement. And *intra*faith conversation must accompany it.

My hope is that congregations, judicatories[326], and individual Christians will increasingly see the need for doing the inner theological work engendered by *inter*faith encounters. Expressions of this need can come from both the grassroots and institutional levels. I also envision every judicatory having an office that deals with *inter*faith issues. Many do, but these are usually involved with dialogues at the institutional level and within cooperative social ministries. This is all well and good, but I would like to see them also provide resources for the average parishioner to experience *inter*faith encounters and explore *intra*faith concerns.

---

[326] A judicatory is the administrative and governing structure of a denomination.

Another dream I have is for seminaries to offer courses dealing with the *intra*faith questions of students as they prepare for parish ministry and perhaps help them prepare for *inter*faith contacts in their future congregations. I have found that, in conversations with seminary students, most are very interested in the theological aspect of this work. Kristin Johnston Largen's most recent book, *Interreligious Learning and Teaching*, validates my experience. In her response to Largen's first chapter, Mary Hess, professor of educational leadership at Luther Seminary, writes,

> "Largen is working off her extensive experience with seminary students in responding to their concerns. I can 'hear' in her chapter the kinds of questions they often raise."[327]

"How Do Christians Talk Among Ourselves about Interfaith Matters?" is a question that is here to stay. In the midst of today's diverse culture, every pastor and church leader should be aware of the Elsies in their congregations. If this question truly is the "next big issue" in the church, it is incumbent upon us to be ready to deal with it. It is my dream to be, not only ready, but excited to be in the conversation. Rather than viewing our diverse world and the issues that arise in it as a "relentless parade," we can instead see the boundless opportunities for creative and imaginative engagement. If we join the parade, we will see all the other visionary and resourceful floats with which we are linked together in a joyous harmony of unity in diversity.

Our float-building is not for ourselves alone. Our future may depend on it. As theologian Hans Küng has famously said:

> No peace among the nations without peace among the religions.

---

[327] Largen, Kristin Johnston, *Interreligious Learning and Teaching*. Minneapolis: Fortress Press, 2014, 37.

No peace among the religions without dialogue between the religions
No dialogue between the religions without investigation of the foundation of the religions.[328]

As we investigate the foundations of Christianity, while at the same time learn about the foundations of others', we will be better able to discern what our float will look like, what symbols we will include and what songs we will sing as we parade by. And in the process, we will make a great contribution to peace-building in our world.

These are my visions and dreams. I am so grateful that you have joined me for this little while in reading this book. Come now and join the parade! I hope to see you there!

---

[328] Küng, Hans, *Christianity: Essence, History, and Future*. New York: Continuum, 1995, 783.

APPENDIX

Appendix A -- A PRAYER

It Is Difficult, O God   by Professor Choan-Seng Song

It is difficult, O God
it was much easier before
we lived in our own world
we took that world for the entire world
we believed we were your chosen people
with special privileges and advantages
we thought we had nothing to learn
from people who were different from us
in what they believed and how they lived
but suddenly all these people are all over the place
they come to live in our midst
they speak all sorts of languages
they practice different faiths
they even dress differently.

It is complicated, O God
it was much simpler in the past
we lived among like-minded people
we used to understand each other
we ate the same food
we shared the common thoughts
we even acquired the same habits
we seldom ventured out of our compound
we were contented with what we knew
but all of a sudden the walls that separated us from other people
crumbled
we have lost control of our life
we are afraid we are no longer master of our own destiny.

But it has never been easy for you, O God
it has never been simple for You
You have always dealt with a world of wonderful plurality
with many people and many nations
with many cultures and religions

with women as well as men
with children as well as men and women.

But instead of complaining, You enjoy it
instead of becoming upset, You delight in it.
Though it is still difficult for us
help us, O God, to enjoy it with all its multiplicity
though it is still too complicated for us
enable us, O God, to cope with it
with the spirit of gratitude and wonder
and inspire us to know ever more deeply
the mystery that is Yours
the truth You alone can disclose to us.

Appendix B -- Rules for Dialogue

GUIDELINES FOR CONVERSATION

It is important to create a safe setting where honest and even painful discussion and struggle can happen. Use the following guidelines to create such a setting.

1. It is important to treat each person with respect.
2. Accept people as they are and where they are in their understanding, even if you disagree with them.
3. Fight the temptation to be absolutely right.
4. Focus on thoughts and feelings, not on questioning people's motives, intelligence, or integrity.
5. Don't be apologetic for what you believe. Say what you think, but in a gentle and loving way.
6. Actively listen and use "I" statements.
7. Agree that it's OK to disagree. Some points will be viewed differently. Keep the discussion open, candid and forthright without intimidating or personally attacking others' positions. Changing one's mind is permitted.
8. Encourage one another to stay in community, even if the discussion is vigorous. Stay as relaxed and connected with each other as possible.
9. Note areas where there is common ground and affirm these.
10. It is OK to stop and reflect. Do not fear moments of silence.
11. Talk with each other, not about each other, before, during or after sessions.
12. Give thanks for the opportunity to talk together.

LISTENING STICK EXERCISE[329]

This exercise is designed to:

- provide an experience of profound listening – to yourself and to others,
- create an awareness of listening and being listened to,
- deepen your respect for each other,
- develop a sense of community.

Divide into small groups of 4 or 5.

Invite someone to be first in each small group. Give this person the listening stick (marking pen, pencil, any small rounded object)

Explain exercise and then demonstrate it.

1. Person who is first states the question to which they will respond (first question is generated in the demonstration). Distinguish answer/response.
2. Reflect on the question (at least 20-30 seconds).
3. Notice your immediate response. Go deeper. Trust your intuition.
4. Speak to your group. Say whatever comes into your mind in response to the question. Take as much time as you need to say what's there to be said.
5. When you're finished, reflect again. Go back inside and ask yourself: "What's the next question that wants to be asked?" It will come to you. This is not a linear exercise; the question may or may not relate to what you've just said. Listen for the question without thought of who will be responding to it.
6. State the question that comes to you and pass the listening stick to the person on your left, who will respond to the new question and repeat the process. The last person to respond

---

[329] The Listening Center, P.O. Box 6805, Laguna Niguel, CA 92607.

is also to generate a question, even though the exercise stops at that point.

Note:

When you're not holding the listening stick, your job is to listen to what each person is saying. It is not a time for you to respond to what has been said or to ask questions. Listen for each other's souls. You may find yourself doing your own reflection in the times of silence. Notice that your response may be very different. Notice how your mind may wander when someone else is speaking. Train yourself to be present. Practice undivided attention.

Debrief:

- When everyone has finished, acknowledge and thank each other. Gather in the large group and reflect on the experience.
- What was it like for you?
- What did you hear?
- What did you notice about the process?

DAVID TRACY'S HARD RULES OF CONVERSATION:[330]

- Say only what you mean
- Say it as accurately as you can
- Listen to and respect what the other says, however different or other
- Be willing to correct or defend your opinions if challenged by the conversation partner
- Be willing to argue if necessary, to confront if demanded, to endure necessary conflict, to change your mind if the evidence suggests it.

---

[330] David Tracy, *Plurality and Ambiguity: Hermeneutics, Religion, and Hope.* NY: Harper & Row, 1987, 19, quoted in Susan M. Simonaitis, "Teaching as Conversation," in *The Scope of Our Art: The Vocation of the Theological Teacher*, ed. L. Gregory Jones and Stephanie Paulsell, 99-119. Grand Rapids: William B. Eerdman's, 2002.

THE EVANGELICAL LUTHERAN CHURCH IN AMERICA:[331]

- Listen as much or more than you talk. Genuine listening is not a passive activity, but an active, demanding one. Listen not only for the content of what is said, but also for the way it is said. Observe carefully the emotion, body language, and other clues about how people are feeling.

- When what someone says makes you uncomfortable, try not to be in a hurry to move on in the conversation. Give the other a full hearing and full consideration.

- State your own thoughts and feelings honestly. Even passionate conversation can be civil and constructive.

- Let people speak for themselves and do not presume to speak for others or know what others believe or think. Therefore, use "I" statements and avoid "You" statements.

- Keep an open mind and heart. Try to understand others as much as possible and be attuned to what you might learn. Try to put yourself in another's place. Look for shared values even though there are serious disagreements.

- Appreciate each other's faith and faithfulness.

- Realize that the Holy Spirit is present and active among all in the conversation. Each participant has a part of the truth you are seeking to discern.

---

[331] ELCA Sexuality Study: "Talking Together as Christians about Tough Social Issues," ELCA Division for Church in Society, 1999.

GUIDELINES FOR INTERFAITH CELEBRATIONS:

For true dialogue to occur it needs to take place within a protective environment of mutually accepted rights and responsibilities, rooted in two fundamental values: respect for the human person and trust in the process of dialogue. Dialogue works best when the participants are willing to develop certain skills that facilitate the process.

Rights	Responsibilities	Skills
1. Each person has the right to define him/herself without being labeled by others	1. Each person must be willing to seriously question his/her assumptions about 'the other'	1. Each person should be able to evaluate and articulate his/her own attitudes, values and positions on issues within the context of his/her tradition
2. Each person has the right to express his or her beliefs, ideas and feelings	2. Each person must allow the same right of self-expression that s/he expects for him/herself	2. Each person should learn how to be more sensitive to what the other is saying
3. Each person has the right to ask questions that help him/her understand what someone else has said	3. Each person should ask questions that respect the other's right of self-definition, even in times of conflict or disagreement	3. Each person should learn how to respond to questions in ways that help others understand
4. Each person has the right not to change or be forced to change	4. Each person must accept the others as equal partners in the dialogue, and acknowledge the dignity of the traditions represented	4. Each person should learn to deal with different points of view while maintaining his/her own integrity
5. Each person has the right to expect that what is said will be held in confidence	5. Each person must agree to hold what others say in confidence	5. Each person should learn to deal with others from a position of mutual trust, based on an expectation that others come to the dialogue in a spirit of honesty and sincerity

[1]   Patrice Brodeur, "Description of the "Guidelines for Interfaith Celebrations,"" in *Journal of Ecumenical Studies*, Vol 34, number 4 (Fall 1997), pp. 559 and 560. The above RRSD is the result of several years of dialogue practice by

BIBLIOGRAPHY

Allen, Ronald J and Clark M. Williamson, *Preaching the Gospels without Blaming the Jews: A Lectionary Commentary*. Louisville, KY: Westminster John Knox Press, 2004.

Ariarajah, S. Wesley, *The Bible and People of Other Faiths*. Geneva: World Council of Churches, 1985.
Not Without My Neighbor: Issues in Interfaith Relations. World Council of Churches, 1999.
Your God, My God, Our God. Geneva, Switzerland: WCC Publications, *2012*.

Armstriong, Karen, *The Great Transformation: The Beginning of Our Religious Traditions*. New York : Alfred A. Knopf, 2006.

Behar, Ruth, *The Vulnerable Observer: Anthropology that Breaks Your Heart*. Boston: Beacon Press, 1996.

Bell, Rob. *Love Wins:* a book about heaven, hell, and the fate of every person who ever lived, New York, NY: HarperOne, 2011.
What We Talk About When We Talk About God, New York, NY: HarperOne, 2014.

Berger, Peter, *A Far Glory: the quest for faith in an age of credulity*. New York: Free Press, 1992.

Berling, Judith, "Getting Out of the Way: A Strategy for Engaging Students in Collaborative Learning," *Teaching Theology & Religion*, Volume 1, Issue 1, page 32, February 1998.
Understanding Other Worlds: A Guide for Interreligious Education. Maryknoll, NY: Orbis Books, 2004.

Berthrong, John H. *The Divine Deli: Religious Identity in the North American Mosaic*. Maryknoll, NY: Orbis Books, 1999.

Beversluis, Joel. *Sourcebook of the World's Religions*. Novato, CA: New World Library, 1993.

Boorstein Sylvia. *That's Funny, You Don't Look Buddhist: On Being a Faithful Jew and a Passionate Buddhist*. San Francisco: HarperSanFrancisco, 1997.

Borg, Marcus and Ross Mackenzie, editors, *God at 2000*. Harrisburg, PA: Morehouse Pub., 2000.

Borg, Marcus, *Jesus: A New Vision*. San Francisco : Harper & Row, 1987.

ed. *Jesus at 2000*. Boulder, CO: Westview Press, 1997.

Meeting Jesus Again for the First Time. San Francisco: HarperSanFrancisco, 1994.

Reading the Bible Again for the First Time. San Francisco: HarperSanFrancisco, 2001.

Speaking Christian: Why Christian Words Have Lost Their Meaning and Power - and How They Can Be Restored. New York : HarperCollins, 2011.

The God We Never Knew. San Francisco, CA: HarperSanFrancisco, 1997.

The Heart of Christianity: Rediscovering a Life of Faith. New York: HarperCollins, 2003.

Bourgeault, Cynthia, *The Wisdom Way of Knowing: Reclaiming an Ancient Tradition to Awaken the Heart*. San Francisco : Jossey-Bass, 2003.

Boys, Mary C. and Sara S. Lee, "The Catholic-Jewish Colloquium: An Experiment in Interreligious Learning," *Religious Education*, v91 n4 p421-66 Fall 1996, 435.

Braybrooke, Marcus, *Faith and Interfaith in a Global Age*. Grand Rapids: CoNexus Press, 1998.

Brelsford, Theodore, "Christological Tensions in a Pluralistic Environment: Managing the Challenges of Fostering and Sustaining Both Identity and Openness." *Religious Education*, 90, no2 (Spring 1995): *174-189*.

Buechner, Frederick, *The Sacred Journey*. San Francisco : Harper & Row, 1982.

Chung, Paul S., *Martin Luther and Buddhism: Aesthetics of Suffering*. Eugene, OR: Wipf and Stock, 2002.

Cobb, John, *Becoming a Thinking Christian*. Nashville: Abingdon Press, 1993.
Beyond Dialogue: Toward a Mutual Transformation of Christianity and Buddhism. Philadelphia: Fortress Press, 1982.
Christ in a Pluralistic Age. Philadelphia: Westminster Press, 1975.
Lay Theology. St. Louis: Chalice Press, 1994.
Transforming Christianity and the World: A Way Beyond Absolutism and Relativism. Maryknoll, NY: Orbis, 1999.
"Responses to Relativism: Common Ground, Deconstruction and Reconstruction," *Soundings*, 73.4 (Winter 1990), 595-6.

Cornille, Catherine, ed., *Many Mansions? Multiple Religious Belonging and Christian Identity*. New York: Orbis Books, 2002.

Countryman, William. *The Mystical Way in the Fourth Gospel: Crossing Over into God*. Valley Forge, PA: Trinity Press International, 1994.

Craine, Renate, *Hildegard: Prophet of the Cosmic Christ*. New York: Crossroad Publishing Company, 1997.

Crossan, John Dominic. *Jesus: A Revolutionary Biography*. San Francisco: HarperSanFrancisco, 1994.

Crossan, John Dominic and Richard G. Watts. *Who Is Jesus?: Answers to Your Questions about the Historical Jesus*. Louisville: Westminster John Knox Press, 1999.

D'Costa, Gavin, *Christianity and the World Religions: Disputed Questions in the Theology of Religions*. Oxford: Blackwell, 2009.
Theology and Religious Pluralism: The Challenge of Other Religions. Oxford: Basil Blackwell, 1986.

Delio, Ilia, "Living in the Ecological Christ," *Franciscan Studies* 64, 2006.

Dunne, John, *The Way of All the Earth*. New York: Macmillan, 1972.

Eck, Diana L. *A New Religious America: How a "Christian Country" Has Become the World's Most Religiously Diverse Nation.* San Francisco: HarperSanFrancisco, 2001.
Encountering God: a spiritual journey from Bozeman to Banaras. Boston: Beacon Press, 1993.

Ehrman, Bart, *Lost Christianities: The Battles for Scripture and the Faiths We Never Knew*. New York: Oxford University Press, 2003.

Farquhar, John, *The Crown of Hinduism.* (London; New York: Humphrey Milford; Oxford University Press, 1915).

Forward, Martin. *Inter-religious Dialogue: A Short Introduction.* Oxford: Oneworld, 2001.

Fox, Matthew, *The Coming of the Cosmic Christ: the healing of Mother Earth and the birth of a global renaissance.* San Francisco: Harper & Row, 1988.
Original Blessing. Santa Fe, N.M.: Bear, 1983.

Funk, Robert, et al. *The Once and Future Jesus.* Santa Rosa, CA: Polebridge Press, 2000.

Gaddy, Welton, "A Strategy for Interfaith Cooperation and Understanding," (lecture presented at the Chautauqua Institution, June 27, 2001), Chautauqua, NY.

Gandhi, Mahatma, "Young India," January 19, 1928.

Gort, Jerald, et al, eds. *Dialogue and Syncretism: An Interdisciplinary Approach.* Grand Rapids: W.B. Eerdmans, 1989.

Griffin, David Ray, ed., *Deep Religious Pluralism.* Louisville, KY: Westminster John Knox Press, 2005.

Hedges, Paul, *Controversies in Interreligious Dialogue and the Theology of Religions.* London, SCM Press. 2010.

Heim, S. Mark. *Salvations: Truth and Difference in Religion*. Maryknoll, NY: Orbis Books, 1995.
Is Christ the Only Way?: Christian Faith in a Pluralistic World. Valley Forge, PA: Judson Press, 1985.

Hick, John. *A Christian Theology of Religions: The Rainbow of Faiths*. Louisville: Westminster John Knox Press, 1995.
God Has Many Names. Philadelphia : Westminster Press, 1982.
The Metaphor of God Incarnate: Christology in a pluralistic age. Louisville, Ky: Westminster John Knox Press, 2006.

Hick, John and Paul F. Knitter, eds. *The Myth of Christian Uniqueness*. Maryknoll, NY: Orbis Books, 1987.

Highland, Chris, *Meditations of John Muir: Nature's Temple*. Birmingham AL: Wilderness Press, 2001.

Hocking, William, Rethinking Missions. New York and London: Harper & Brothers, 1932.

Hunt, Rex A. E. and John W.H. Smith, *Why Weren't We Told?* Farmington, MN: Polbridge Press, 2013.

Huxley, Aldous. *The Perennial Philosophy*. London: Chatto & Windus, 1957.

Inbody, Tyrone, *The Many Faces of Christology*. Nashville: Abingdon Press, 2002.

Isherwood, Lisa, *Liberating Christ : exploring the christologies of contemporary liberation movement*. Cleveland, Ohio : Pilgrim Press, 1999.

Johnson, Kurt and David Robert Ord, *The Coming Interspiritual Age*. Vancouver: Namaste Publishing, 2013.

Kaplan, Stephen, *Different Paths, Different Summits*. Lanham, MD: Rowman & Littlefield Publishers, Inc., 2002.

Kearney, Richard. *Anatheism (Returning to God after God)*. New York: Columbia University Press, 2011.

Kimball Charles, *When Religion Becomes Evil*. NY: Harper Collins, 2002.

Knitter, Paul. *No Other Name? A Critical Survey of Christian Attitudes toward the Worlds Religions*. Maryknoll, NY: Orbis Books, 1985. *Without Buddha I Could Not Be a Christian*. Oxford: Oneworld, 2009.

Kraemer, Hendrik, *The Christian Message in a Non-Christian World*. New York: Harper and Row, 1938, 107.

Kung, Hans, *Christianity: Essence, History, and Future*. New York: Continuum, 1995.
Theology for the Third Millennium. New York: Doubleday, 1988.

Largen, Kristir. Johnston, *Finding God Among Our Neighbors: An Interfaith Systematic Theology*. Minneapolis: Fortress Press, 2013. *Interreligious Learning and Teaching*. Minneapolis: Fortress Press, 2014.

Magida, Arthur, J. *How to Be a Perfect Stranger: A Guide to Etiquette in Other People's Religious Ceremonies, Volumes 1 and 2*. Woodstock, VT: Jewish Lights Publications, 1995-1997.

Maloney, George A., *Abiding in the Indwelling Trinity*. Mahwah, NJ: Paulist Press, 2005.
Entering Into the Heart of Jesus. NY: Alba House, 1988.
The Cosmic Christ: From Paul to Teilhard. New York: Sheed and Ward, 1968.

Marty, Martin, "This We Can Believe: A Pluralistic Vision." *Religious Education* 75 (January-February 1980): 37- 49.

McFague, Sallie, *The Body of God*. Minneapolis, MN: Fortress Press, 1993.
Models of God. Philadelphia: Fortress Press, 1987.

McLaren, Brian D., *Why Did Jesus, Moses, the Buddha, and Mohammed Cross the Road?: Christian Identity in a Multi-Faith World*. New York: Jericho Books, 2012.

Merigan, Terrance, "Religious Knowledge in the Pluralist Theology of Religions," *Theological Studies*, 58, 1997.

Min, Anselm, "Dialectical Pluralism and Solidarity of Others: Towards a New Paradigm." *Journal of the American Academy of Religions*, Fall97, Vol. 65 Issue 3, p587.

Moyaert, Marianne. *Fragile Identities: Towards a Theology of Interreligious Hospitality*. Amsterdam: Rodopi B.V., 2011.

Nah, David S., "A Critical Evaluation Of John Hick's Theology Of Religious Pluralism" A Dissertation submitted to the Faculty of Claremont Graduate University in partial fulfillment of the requirements for the degree of Doctor of Philosophy in the Graduate Faculty of Religion, Claremont, CA, 2005.

Niebuhr, Gustav, *Beyond Tolerance: Searching for Interfaith Understanding in America*. New York: Viking, 2008.

Panikkar, Raimundo, "Christian Identity in a Time of Pluralism." *Pacific Coast Theological Society Papers 1939-1999,* Nov. 19-20, 1976.
The Intrareligious Dialogue. New York: Paulist Press, 1978.

Peace, Jennifer Howe, Or N. Rose, and Gregory Mobley, editors, *My Neighbor's Faith : stories of interreligious encounter, growth, and transformation*. Maryknoll, NY: Orbis Books, 2012.

Price, Lynn, *Interfaith Encounter and Dialogue*. New York: P. Lang, 1991.

Priests for Equality, *The Inclusive Bible: The First Egalitarian Translation*. Lanham, Md.: Rowman & Littlefield Publishers, 2007.

Prothero, Stephen, *God Is Not One: the eight rival religions that run the world-- and why their differences matter*. NY: HarperCollins, 2011.

Race, Alan, *Christians and Religious Pluralism: Patterns in the Christian Theology of Religions.* London: SCM Press, 1983.

Roberts, Alexander and James Donaldson, editors, "The Arabic Infancy Gospel of the Savior" in *The Ante-Nicene Fathers Volume 8.* Grand Rapids, MI: W.B. Eerdmans, 1985-1987.

Samartha, S. J. *One Christ – Many Religions: Toward a Revised Christology.* Maryknoll, NY: Orbis Books, 1991.

Sanguin, Bruce, *Darwin, Divinity and the Dance of the Cosmos.* Kelowna, BC: CopperHouse, 2007.
If Darwin Prayed: Prayers for Evolutionary Mystics. evans and sanguin publishing, 2010.
 The Emerging Church- A Model for Change and a Map for Renewal. Kelowna, BC: CopperHouse, 2014.

Savary, Louis M., *Teilhard de Chardin - The Divine Milieu Explained: A Spirituality for the 21st Century.* Mahwah, NJ: Paulist Press, 2007.

Schuon, Fritjof. *The Transcendent Unity of Religions.* New York: Harper & Row, 1975.

Seymour, Jack L. and Donald E. Miller. *Theological Approaches to Christian Education.* Nashville: Abingdon Press, 1990.

Shaku, Soyen, *Zen for Americans.* Translated by Daisetz Teitaro Suzuki, La Salle, Ill., Open Court [1974, c1906].

Shapiro, Rami, *Perennial Wisdom for the Spiritually Independent.* Woodstock, VT: SkyLight Paths, 2013.

Simonaitis, Susan M. "Teaching as Conversation." In *The Scope of Our Art: The Vocation of the Theological Teacher*, ed. L. Gregory Jones and Stephanie Paulsell, 99-119. Grand Rapids: William B. Eerdman's, 2002.

Siejk, Kate. "Wonder: The Creative Condition for Interreligious Dialogue." *Religious Education* (Spring 1995): 227-240.

Smith, Huston. *The Illustrated World's Religions: A Guide to Our Wisdom Traditions.* HarperOne; 1st HarperCollins Pbk. Ed edition, 1995.

Song, Choan-Seng. *The Believing Heart: An Invitation to Story Theology.* Minneapolis: Fortress Press, 1999.
What Is Christian Mission?: Starting Again with Jesus
ed. *Doing Theology Today.* Madras: Christian Literature Society, 1976.

Spong, John Shelby. *Why Christianity Must Change or Die : A Bishop Speaks to Believers in Exile: A New Reformation of the Church's Faith and Practice.* San Francisco: HarperSanFrancisco, 1998.
and Lucy Newton Boswell Negus, *Christpower.* Haworth, NJ: Saint Johann Press, 2007.

Standaert, Benoit, *Sharing Sacred Space: Interreligious Dialogue as Spiritual Encounter.* Collegeville, MN: Liturgical Press, 2009.

Stedman, Chris, *Faitheist: how an atheist found common ground with the religious.* Boston: Beacon Press, 2012.

Stendahl, Krister, "From God's Perspective We Are All Minorities," (Note: Text based on a lecture delivered on February 27, 1992, at the Center for the Study of World Religions, Harvard University, as edited by Arvind Sharma and Jennifer Baichwal).

Strouse, Susan M., "Passing Over and Coming Back: What Does It Mean to Be a Christian in an Interfaith World?" (doctor of ministry thesis, Pacific School of Religion, 2005).

Suchocki, Marjorie Hewitt. *God-Christ-Church: A Practical Guide to Process Theology.* New York: Crossroad Publishing Co., 1986.
Divinity & Diversity: A Christian Affirmation of Religious Pluralism. Nashville: Abingdon Press, 2003.

Swidler, Leonard, "The Age of Global Dialogue," *Marburg Journal of Religion:* Volume 1, No. 2 (July 1996).

Teasdale, Wayne. *The Mystic Heart: Discovering a Universal Spirituality in the World's Religions*. Novato, CA: New World Library, 1999.

Teilhard de Chardin, Pierre, *Hymn of the Universe*. New York: Harper & Row, 1969, 1965.
The Phenomenon of Man. New York: Harper & Row, 1959.
Writings in Time of War. New York: Harper & Row, 1968.

Teilhard de Chardin. Pierre and Ursula King. *Teilhard de Chardin: Writings (Modern Spiritual Masters Series)*. Maryknoll, NY: Orbis Books, 1999.

Tickle, Phyllis, *The Great Emergence: How Christianity Is Changing and Why*. Grand Rapids, Mich.: Baker Books, 2008.

Tillich, Paul. *Christianity and the Encounter of the World's Religions*. New York: Columbia University Press, 1963.

Tracy, David. *Dialogue with the Other: The Interreligious Dialogue*. Grand Rapids, MI: Eerdman's, 1991.
The Analogical Imagination: Christian Theology and the Culture of Pluralism. NY: Crossroad, 1981.

Trent, J. Dana, *Saffron Cross: The Unlikely Story of How a Christian Minister Married a Hindu Monk*. Nashville, TN: Fresh Air Books, 2013.

Troeltsch, Ernst, "The Place of Christianity Among the World Religions" in *Christian Thought: Its History and Application*, edited by Baron von Hügel. NY: Meridian Books, 1957, 35-63.

ACKNOWLEDGEMENTS

I wish to thank all those who have been wise guides and helpers along the road to publication of this book: Rev. Megan Rohrer, who put in many hours of editing, designing, and formatting; Dr. Kathleen Hurty, friend, mentor, and encourager; Linda Crawford, friend and fellow Enneagram "One;" Paul and Jan Chaffee, who quickly engaged me in interfaith work in the Bay Area on my arrival; the people of First United Lutheran Church; and of course, Laurence Schechtman, my #1 fan. And in memorium: Elsie Leary of North Park Lutheran Church in Buffalo, NY, who started me off on this journey which I have always called "the Elsie Project" in her honor.

It would be impossible to name all the wonderful friends and colleagues who have contributed to my *inter*faith and *intra*faith education. I hope they know how deeply grateful I am to all of them and how much I look forward to continuing this work together.

56914123R00126

Made in the USA
Lexington, KY
02 November 2016